CUSTOM
CLOSETS
Organize & Build

Manufactured in the United States of America

Creative Director: Warren Ramezzana
Editor: Kimberly Kerrigone
Graphic Designer: Annie Jeon
Photo Researcher: Kimberly Kerrigone
Illustrators: Herb Hughes, James Randolph
Electronic Production: Annie Jeon, Mindy Circelli,
    Warren Ramezzana
Technical Reviewer: Jim Barrett

Cover Design: Warren Ramezzana
Cover Photograph: Decourage Ltd./George Kopp

Electronic Prepress: M. E. Aslett Corporation

Current Printing (last digit)
10 9 8 7 6 5 4 3 2

Custom Closets: Organize & Build
LC: 92-74446
ISBN: 1-880029-03-0 (paper)

CREATIVE HOMEOWNER PRESS®
A Division of Federal Marketing Corp.
24 Park Way
Upper Saddle River, NJ 07458

Photography Credits:

Alumax, 15, back cover
Closet Maid, Clairson International, 5 (top), 6 (bottom),
    7, 10 (top), 14 (middle), back cover
Everette Short, 3, 6, 9
Herb Hughes, 4
Hirsh, 5 (bottom), 14 (top)
Lee/Rowan, 10 (bottom)
Melabee M. Miller, 8, back cover
Osage Products Co., 14 (bottom)
Phillip H. Ennis Photography, 1, 16, back cover
Shulte, 11 (top)
Stack-A-Shelf, AFCO Industries, Inc., 6 (bottom left)
Sturdi-Craft, 11 (bottom)
Tamor Plastics Corporation, 13
Techline, 12, back cover

We would like to thank Closet Maid for the use of the Carousel-Style Closet project, 63-67.

Safety First

Though all the designs and methods in this book have been tested for safety, it is not possible to overstate the importance of using the safest methods possible. What follows are reminders; some do's and don'ts. They are not substitutes for your own common sense.

Use caution, care, and good judgment when following the procedures described in this book.

Check local building codes when planning new construction. The codes are intended to protect your safety and should be observed to the letter.

Always wear eye protection.

Wear the appropriate gloves when handling chemicals, heavy construction or when sanding.

Wear a disposable mask when working with odors, dust or mist.

Be sure that the electrical setup is safe; be sure that circuits are not overloaded and that all power tools and electrical outlets are properly grounded. Do not use power tools in wet locations.

Be aware that there is never time for your body's reflexes to save you from injury from a power tool; everything happens too fast. Be alert!

Read container labels on paints, solvents, and other products. Provide ventilation, and observe all other warnings.

Know the limitations of your tools. Do not try to force them to do what they were not designed to do. Read manufacturer's instructions.

Do not change a blade or a bit unless the power cord is unplugged. Do not depend on the switch being off; you might accidently turn it on.

Use holders or pushers to work pieces shorter than three inches on a table saw or jointer. Whenever possible, cut small pieces off of larger pieces.

Do not wear loose clothing, hanging hair, open cuffs, or jewelry while working.

Keep your hands away from the business ends of blades, cutters and bits. Hold a portable circular saw with both hands so that you know where your hands are at all times.

Do not support a workpiece with your leg or any other part of your body when sawing or drilling. Clamp small pieces firmly to a work surface.

Do not carry sharp or pointed tools; use a special-purpose tool belt with leather pockets and holders instead.

Flammable or volatile materials such as paints and finishes should only be stored in approved storage containers. Never store flammable liquids near radiators, heating units, fireplaces, chimneys or flues; or near any electrical equipment.

Contents

What are Your Closet Needs?

This is the book that will show you how to achieve a suitable closet once and for all. If you are like most people, there never seems to be enough closet space. The key to a workable closet, no matter what the size, is organization. With this book as a guide, you will learn the best way in which to achieve an organized closet. If your closet is already organized, and yet, you still seem to be lacking space, then you need to expand the closet that exists or build a new one. If this is your situation, you are in luck, this book shows how to construct a closet from scratch as well.

Custom Closets features 14 projects. The first eight consist of organization projects. You will find a variety of models which cater to the specific needs of men, women and children. Install one of the organizers you see here, or pick and choose certain aspects from different projects to create a custom design of your own. The remaining six projects feature building new closet space. Whether you would like to broaden your existing closet or add a new reach-in, walk-in or freestanding closet, you will find full, step-by-step instructions that show you how.

Also included in the book is a guide which details some of the construction techniques you will use while working on these projects. From toenailing boards to installing clips and hooks, all the basics you need to know are found here.

Before

After

Design & Organize

You can increase the storage capacity of most standard closets by 50 to 75 percent or more just by adding an organizer system. No matter how tightly packed, most single rod and shelf closets contain a lot of unused volume. By organizing the area, you can take advantage of that volume, greatly increasing storage and, at the same time, placing things within reach. You can accomplish this by installing a shelf tower with or without drawers, hanging rods, hooks, shelves, and other storage specialty devices. These items make it possible for you to keep often used objects within easy reach and less-used objects stored neatly away.

Origins of Organization

Closet organization is by no means a new idea. Decades, even centuries ago, the function of a closet was served by a highly organized piece of furniture. This freestanding closet, or wardrobe, was built to meet the owner's needs. Its main purpose was to maximize storage within a reasonable amount of space. As houses became more of an "assembly-line" affair, closets were built into the home. At the time, the additional square footage in a home was less expensive than the cost of buying a new wardrobe unit. This was the beginning of the single rod and shelf closet.

As time passed, the cost of homes per square foot began to rise dramatically. At the same time, most people began to collect more clothing than ever before. There also became a need to store a myriad of other materials. Hence, closet organization became a popular means for getting more storage in less space.

Closet Options

In recent years, closet organization has become quite like a form of art. Depending upon your situation and your storage needs, there are many ways in which a closet can be arranged. Decisions from how many shelves to include to whether you would like a homemade or commercially built system must be addressed. The closet organizer system will vary depending upon whether the closet is being used by a man or a woman or both; whether the user is an adult or a child; and whether the closet is a reach-in or walk-in.

The system must be scaled to the user. For children, in-season items should be stored at a lower level so that kids can reach things themselves. Along the same lines, an individual who is six feet tall may have a problem with items that are stored two feet off the floor. For a tall person, design the organizer to locate commonly used items at a higher level. If a member of the family is physically disabled, you will need to design the closet for easy access. Someone in a wheelchair will not be able to reach items stored above a specific height.

Study Your Closet Needs

Use this list of eight easy steps to assess your current household closet situation and what you can do to make it better.

1. Study the storage habits and needs of the entire family.

2. List all items to be stored.

3. Determine what can be discarded or donated to charity to reduce the amount of closet space needed.

4. Make a storage list for each room (out-of-season items can be moved to a different area, such as an attic or storage room).

5. Use the information detailed on the following pages to determine the amount of closet space required in each room.

6. Calculate whether the current closets can be organized to gain the needed space, or if additional space will be required.

7. If additional space is needed, determine where it will be located and the size and type of space required.

8. Design the organizer system best suited for each closet.

Plan Ahead

A great deal of effort goes into shopping for and installing a closet organizer. If you decide to organize a closet without taking the time to assess your needs, you can be sure that you will run into some problems. If you have not planned accurately, you may finish the job and find that you still are not able to fit all of your clothing and other items. On the other hand, you may overestimate the amount of space you need and get more than you bargained for. This is not as severe a problem as being short on storage and, in some cases, this situation may be desirable. If, however, you sacrificed part of a room to add a new or expanded closet and now the room is too cramped, you will regret the time and expense. Both problems can be avoided by calculating in advance how much storage you actually need.

How much space do you actually need? While it could take several hours to calculate the answer to this question, doing so is a very important step. Take stock of your possessions, and plan the space to accommodate them. Don't forget to set aside space for possessions you plan to acquire in the future.

How Much Hanging Space?

Men's Clothing Chart	W	L
Jacket	2"	45"
Long Coat	2¼"	60"
Bathrobe	1½"	54"
Suit	2½"	42"
Slacks Over Hanger	1½"	39"
Slacks—Cuff Clip	1"	54"
Shirt	1¼"	39"

Women's Clothing Chart	W	L
Jacket	2"	36"
Short Coat	2"	42"
Long Coat	2¼"	60"
Bathrobe	1½"	51"
Dress	2"	60"
Skirts	1¾"	36"
Slacks Over Hanger	1½"	36"
Slacks—Cuff Clip	1"	51"
Blouse	1¼"	36"

The width and length measurements found on the charts above can be adjusted for short or tall people as necessary. Keep in mind, the widths may have to be adjusted to accommodate thicker or thinner styles and materials. Take into account any special hanging needs that you might have (such as ski outfits which take up more space). Plan ahead for future additions to the wardrobe by adding 10 to 15 percent to the calculated length of any hanging rod. Then figure the total number of lineal inches needed for each item's height. Different types of items that are similar lengths may, of course, be grouped together. Use the tallest height for the entire group.

How Much Shelf Space?

Determine the amount of shelf space that you will need by accounting for the amount of shoes, linens and clothing that is not hung or enclosed in a dresser. Remember to add a cushion of 10 to 15 percent to the total shelf space needed. Avoid designing the closet with items placed on the floor. This makes it difficult to keep the floor clean. Some items, such as jeans, sweats and jackets may be hung from hooks. If this type of storage suits you, be sure to design a space for hanging hooks.

How Much Drawer Space?

If you have a number of items that you would like to keep out of view or simply in an enclosed space, consider installing a shelf tower with drawers. Determine how many drawers you would like and how large they should be. A tower also provides a convenient space for hanging hooks. Shorter systems, particularly coated-wire drawer systems, may be installed with casters so that you can roll it from place to place if necessary.

Getting the Job Done

The amount of money you would like to spend on your new organizer system is an important consideration that may dictate the approach you should take.

The most cost-efficient method is to plan the project yourself, purchase the organizer system at a discount building material store, then install the system yourself. For an average-size, 6-foot closet this can cost from $100-$500 (depending on the complexity of the design and the type of material you are working with). Installing a hand-built system could cost less, but it also requires more labor.

An alternative to installing the system yourself is to hire a carpenter to install the system for you. Make sure you are dealing with a reputable contractor and that all agreements are written and signed.

You may choose to visit a specialty closet store which concentrates on closet organization. These shops provide an in-home analysis, and then develop and install the organizer for you. Some stores will provide this full service for not much more than the cost of the materials. However, not all specialty shops are quite so reasonable.

If your budget allows, you can visit a closet designer, an individual akin to both an architect and interior designer. This, of course, is the most expensive way to go. If the design includes custom cabinets with complicated woodwork, the cost may be quite substantial.

angers

There are many individual pieces that can be purchased to help organize your closet. The following do not require installation.

Double-Hanging Rod

Several gadgets that turn a regular single rod and shelf closet into a double-hanging closet are available. The principle is simple: Two lengths of material (metal, coated-wire, plastic) hang from the regular closet rod. At the bottom, there is a rod that connects them. Clothes hang from this rod, as well as from the original closet rod above.

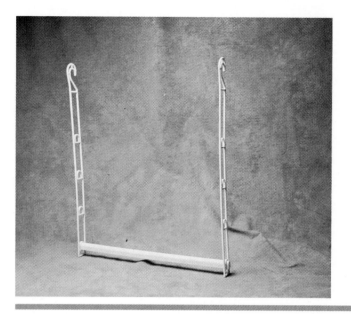

Slack Hangers

The slack hanger has been around for decades. This hanger allows you to store a number of pairs of pants in a space not much wider than would normally be required by one pair. The only drawback is that it is harder to get a pair of slacks on and off the hanger.

Tie & Belt Racks

Tie and belt racks are available in numerous styles. Different types include those that hang directly from the closet rod or from the door; those that are installed on a bare wall; and freestanding units that rotate for easier access.

Hanging Shelf Tower

This device is a simple alternative to a shelf tower that is built into an organizer system. The hanging unit has one advantage over the rest in that it can be moved or removed with little effort. A disadvantage is that it cannot hold as much weight.

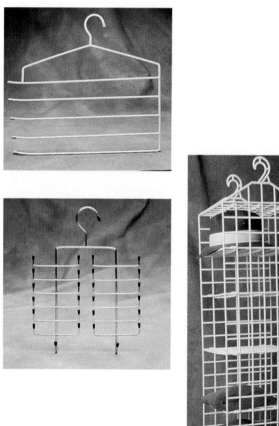

hoe Racks

There are probably more types of shoe racks than any other type of organizer. This includes units that can be hung from the closet rod, hung over the door, mounted on the back of the door, mounted on the wall, or simply placed on the floor. Materials used to make shoe racks include metal rods, steel wire, vinyl, quilted cloth, wood, particleboard, and plastic. Study your needs and habits, then buy or build the type of shoe rack that suits you the best.

torage Boxes

The market is loaded with wood, particleboard, and cardboard boxes that provide open or closed storage. Some of these are decorated with prints. Though the cardboard boxes are engineered to be quite strong, there are limits to what they can support. Assembling the boxes can be tricky no matter what the material, so take care when putting them together.

edar Lining

Not only is cedar an attractive wood, it also retains a unique moth-deterring aroma, perfect for use inside a clothes closet. Cedar also is highly resistant to decay.

Build & Expand

If it is not possible to organize an existing closet to meet your needs, you may wish to build a new closet. Determine the location of the new closet. Then, decide whether you would like it to be a walk-in or a reach-in. Finally, determine how large the closet should be.

When locating a new closet, keep the following in mind: The items to be stored must be close to the area in which they will be used. If the closet's main purpose is to store clothing, obviously it should be placed in the bedroom or dressing room. Next,

before purchasing materials, draw a detailed plan. Be sure to take note of room specifics, such as traffic patterns, size and shape of the room, free wall space, and the furniture that exists. Last, check the amount of space that will remain in the room. Do not compromise a room so severely that it becomes uncomfortable to the user.

Study your home to determine your closet needs, then study the construction projects in this book to find the organizer system that best fulfills those needs.

His Reach-In Closet

This organizer is designed to accommodate the needs of a man who has his own closet and would like to store both casual wear and dress clothes. Even a closet that is only 5 feet wide can be carefully organized to handle a man's storage needs, however a 6-foot-wide closet is more comfortable. For closets that are less than 5-feet wide, eliminate the shelf-tower system. For very wide closets (10 feet or more) consider customizing a more elaborate design.

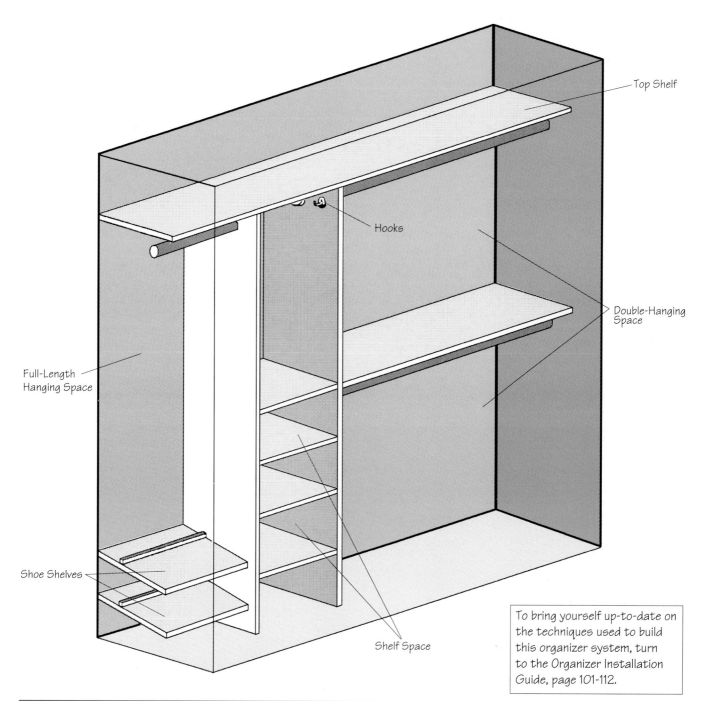

Top Shelf

Hooks

Double-Hanging Space

Full-Length Hanging Space

Shoe Shelves

Shelf Space

To bring yourself up-to-date on the techniques used to build this organizer system, turn to the Organizer Installation Guide, page 101-112.

Hand-Built Organizer

Time Required:	Novice	Average	Experienced
	12 Hrs.	8 Hrs.	4 Hrs.

Tools & Materials

☐ Variable Speed Drill with Screwdriver Bit or Screwdriver
☐ Hammer
☐ Combination Square
☐ Pencil
☐ Table Saw (Optional)
☐ Level
☐ Crosscut (Hand) Saw
☐ 1x4 (If needed at back wall)
☐ 1¼" Wood Screws
☐ 2d Finishing Nails
☐ Measuring Tape
☐ Framing Square
☐ Utility Knife
☐ Circular Saw
☐ Miter Saw
☐ Paint or Stain
☐ Hanging Rod (As needed)
☐ 4d Finishing Nails
☐ Carpenter's Glue
☐ 1x1 Or Smaller Stock For Heel Stop (Optional)
☐ (2) Sheets 3/4" Plywood (Cut into 3 strips, 16" wide)
☐ 1x2 Furring - 1x1 or 45-degree Trim May Be Used (As needed)
☐ (12') 1x4 - Clear Grade or Number 1 Grade

NOTE: *If the organizer is not going to be painted the same color as the closet, paint or stain it before installing, and then touch up afterward. This will be much easier than trying to paint precise lines where the organizer meets the closet walls.*

1 Select & Cut Plywood

The first step in building the organizer is to obtain the wood for the project. A guide to selecting and cutting plywood is found on page 101.

2 Build & Install Shelf Tower

Cut two strips of plywood to 83¼" long. Determine the shelf arrangement you want, then multiply the number of shelves by two and cut as many 12"-long 1x2 furring strips. (You can also use 1x1 or 45-degree trim for the furring strips.) Cut the shelves to 1½" less than the desired width of the shelf tower. The design for this project shows an 18"-wide shelf tower, which means the shelves will be cut to 16½"-wide. Determine the width of your shelf tower based on closet width and the amount of items to be stored on shelves. Construct the shelf tower as detailed on page 102-105.

Measure 18" from the left side wall and place a mark on the back wall of the closet. Use a level to draw a plumb, vertical line through the mark. As detailed on page 105, add two furrings strips to the back of the tower, at the top and bottom, and secure to the wall with plastic anchors and wood screws. Before securing the tower, however, measure the width of the closet at the 84" height and cut a shelf to that length from a 16"-wide strip of plywood. Set the shelf in place but do not secure, then secure the shelf tower. This is necessary because the top shelf may be difficult or impossible to install after the shelf tower is secure.

If the closet is more than 8' wide, the top shelf will have to be installed in two pieces. The seam should be directly above the seam between the right side of the shelf tower and the rod and shelf support. This should be done after the shelf tower is secured. Do not secure the top shelf at this time.

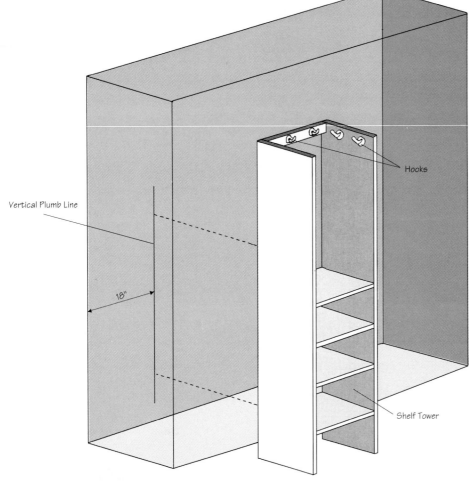

Vertical Plumb Line

18"

Hooks

Shelf Tower

Install Shelf Tower

3 *Install Rod & Shelf Supports*

Measure up 44¼" from the floor on the right side of the shelf tower. Use a level to draw a line along the right side of the tower at the mark. Continue the line along the back wall of the closet and wrap it around the right side wall. Use the level again to extend the line of the top of the shelf tower around the back wall and onto the right side wall.

On the left side of the closet draw another line from the top of the shelf tower around to the left side wall. If not installing shoe shelves, draw a line on the left side of the shelf tower, back wall, and left side wall at 65¼" and 74¼" from the floor.

Cut and install three pairs of rod and shelf supports as detailed on page 101. Each pair should have a 16"-long support as well as a support as long as the closet is deep. Install two pairs on the right side of the closet at the level lines. On the left side, install the third pair of rod and shelf supports at the single level line if installing shoe shelves. If not installing shoe shelves install the rod and shelf supports at the lower of the three level lines. Install 1x2 furring strips at the other two lines. If the hanging space on the right side is wider than 4', install a 1x4 on the back wall at the level lines.

4 *Install Rods*

Measure the distance from the right side wall to the shelf tower at the lower pair of supports. Cut a length of rod to fit and insert one end into the support with the drilled hole only. Slide the other end into the slot cut in the opposite support. Repeat for the upper rod, then for the left side rod.

Install Rods & Shelves

5 *Install Shelves*

Turn to pages 102-104 for details on building and installing wooden, hand-built shelves (see illustration page 17 for placement). Remember the top shelf should be secured last.

6 *Install Shoe Shelves*

Turn to page 107 for details on building and installing wooden, hand-built shoe shelves.

7 *Attach Trim Strips to Plywood*

Turn to page 103 for details on trimming the plywood.

Laminate Organizer

Time Required:	Novice 4 Hrs.	Average 3 Hrs.	Experienced 1.5 Hrs.

Tools & Materials (May vary depending on manufacturer.)

☐ Variable Speed Drill with Screwdriver Bit or Screwdriver

☐ Hammer ☐ Measuring Tape

☐ Pencil ☐ Level

☐ (1 or 2) Shelf Towers ☐ Shelf Tower

☐ Hooks ☐ (3) Adjustable Rods

☐ (2) 18" Shoe Shelves

☐ (2) Shelves (Additional shelf optional)

Hardware Needed (If not included in shelf tower kit):

☐ (2) Angle Brackets ☐ (4) Plastic Anchors

☐ (4) 1" Wood Screws ☐ (4) 3/4" Wood Screws

NOTE: *Instructions for the installation of laminated systems are manufacturer specific. Only general instructions are given here.*

1 Install Shelf Tower

This project includes shelves in the lower half of the tower and hanging hooks in the upper half. For details on laminated shelf towers, turn to page 108.

Measure 18" from the left side of the closet and place a mark. Use a level to draw a vertical line at the mark. Assemble the shelf tower per the manufacturer's directions and set in place in the closet with the left side on the line drawn on the back wall. Secure to the back wall following the manufacturer's directions, if provided. If not, secure with two angle brackets as detailed on page 108.

2 Install Rods

The adjustable hanging rods used with laminated organizer systems come in different sizes. Common sizes include a small rod that adjusts from 18" to 30" and a large rod that adjusts from 30" to 48", though what you find may differ. Use a rod adjustable to 18" on the left side and install per the manufacturer's directions at 67" above the floor if you are not going to install a shoe rack and at 82" above the floor if you are installing a shoe rack. Use a level when installing the rod. The distance from the closet back wall to the rod is based on the depth of the closet as shown in the following chart.

Closet Depth	Dimension
23" or More	12"
20" to 23"	1/2 Closet Depth
20 " or Less	10"

On the right side, the size rod you purchase will depend on the size of your closet and the width of the shelf tower. Measure the width from the right side wall to the right side of the shelf tower at 43" and 82" above the floor. The width at two different locations could vary since walls are often not plumb. Install rods of the appropriate size adjusted to the required length at the two heights.

3 Install Shelves

A shelf above the rod on the right and above the top rod will provide additional space for folded clothes, hats, and other items. Determine the exact shelf arrangement, measure the length of the shelves, then cut and install per the manufacturer's directions. If you are not adding shoe shelves on the left, you can substitute an additional rod and shelf.

4 Install Shoe Shelves

If you opt for laminate shoe shelves, see page 108.

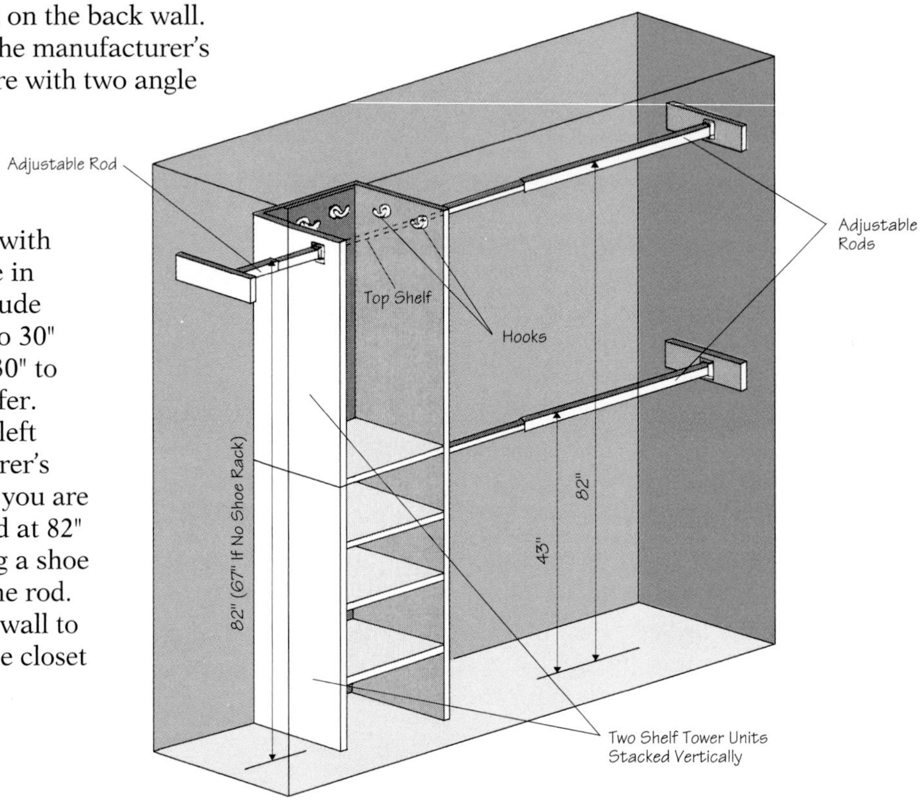

Install Shelf Tower & Rods

Coated-Wire Organizer

Time Required:	Novice	Average	Experienced
	3 Hrs.	2 Hrs.	1 Hr.

Tools & Materials

- ☐ Variable Speed Drill with Screwdriver Bit or Screwdriver
- ☐ Hammer
- ☐ Pencil
- ☐ Measuring Tape
- ☐ Level
- ☐ Bolt Cutters or Hacksaw
- ☐ 12" Rod and Shelf (As needed)
- ☐ 16" Rod and Shelf (As needed)
- ☐ (3') 12" Organizer Shelf
- ☐ (26) Small End Caps
- ☐ (8) Large End Caps
- ☐ (1) 7-Runner Side Frame Set
- ☐ (1) Cross Brace Set
- ☐ Wire-Basket Drawers
- ☐ Drawer Stops (As needed)
- ☐ (1) Set Casters (Optional)
- ☐ (3) End Brackets
- ☐ (2) Sets Shoe Shelf Supports
- ☐ Back Clips
- ☐ Down Clips
- ☐ Screws
- ☐ Plastic Anchors
- ☐ Hooks
- ☐ (1) Set Floor Protectors (If not using casters)
- ☐ (1) Set Leg Extensions (For casters)
- ☐ (1) Drawer System Top (Optional)
- ☐ 12" Support Braces (As needed)
- ☐ Joiner Plate Assemblies (As needed)

1 Install Back Clips

Turn to organizers page 109-110, for a detailed look at a variety of clips and how to install them.

Measure 45" and 84" (adjust for the height of the user) up from the floor at the right corner of the closet and place marks on the back wall. At the 45" mark use a level to draw a horizontal line along the back wall to 36" from the left side, if using a 17"-wide drawer system, and 41" from the left side if using a 22"-wide drawer system. Use the level again at the higher mark, drawing a horizontal line from wall to wall.

Starting with either line, make a mark 5/8" above the line and 2½" from the right side. Continue making marks 5/8" above the line and 12" apart until you reach the opposite end of the shelf line (2½" from the left wall for the top line). Complete this process for both lines. Install a back clip at each of the marks for hollow or masonry walls. For wood walls at least 1" thick, use down clips.

2 Install Rods & Shelves

Measure the length of the upper shelf. Use bolt cutters to cut a piece of 16"-wide integral rod and shelf to the measured length less 1½". (You also can cut the shelf with a hacksaw, but it takes

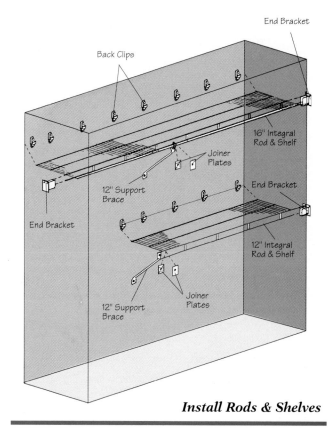

Install Rods & Shelves

considerably longer. Many building supply dealers will cut the shelf materials to the length you specify at the time of purchase.) Slide end caps over the cut ends of the steel wires. The two steel wires that make up the clothes hanging part of the shelf require large end caps. The other three wires use small end caps.

Snap the shelf into place by following the directions found on page 110 (top left).

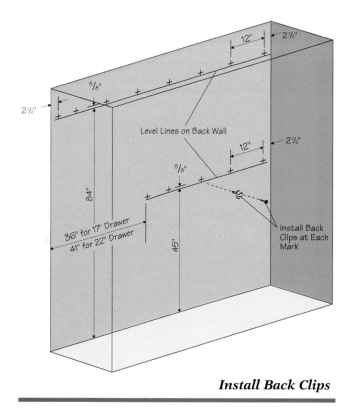

Install Back Clips

At the lower line, measure the length of the shelf and cut a 12" integral rod and shelf to the measured length less 3/4". Slide end caps onto the cut ends of the wires. Again, the two steel wires that make up the clothes hanging part of the shelf require large end caps. Snap into place as before. Install an end bracket at the right side wall and a 12" support brace at the left end of the shelf (see page 110). If the shelf is longer than 3½', install an additional support brace every 3½', starting from the side wall on the right.

3 Install Wire-Basket Drawer System

Assemble the wire-basket drawer system as detailed on page 112. Set in place at the end of the lower rod and shelf as shown.

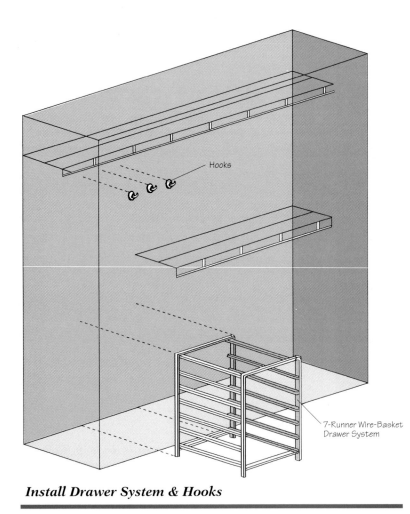

Hooks

7-Runner Wire-Basket
Drawer System

Install Drawer System & Hooks

4 Install Hooks or Second Drawer System

Install the hooks for ties, belts and other items as detailed on page 112.

If you prefer, you can stack an additional drawer system on top of the first. For stacked drawer systems buy two 7-runner systems or a 10-runner and a 4-runner system. Do not exceed 14 runners. The drawers would be too high to reach. Build one frame without the top cross braces, then tap the L connectors in the bottom of a second frame into the top of the first frame. Slide the stacked drawer system into place in the closet. Do NOT put casters on a stacked drawer system. While it will rest in the closet without any problems, two units high is not stable enough to be mobile.

5 Install Shoe Shelves

If you would like to install wire-coated shoe shelves, follow the instructions found on page 111 (see page 17 for placement).

Build Your Own Tie Rack

First determine the length of the rack and cut a piece of 1-by stock to that length. Sand until smooth. Purchase and install hooks or drill holes for wood dowels. Be sure the holes are drilled straight. If installing dowels, use a wood drill bit equal in diameter to the dowel. Apply glue to the dowel and insert into the drilled hole. Clean any excess glue. Attach the rack to the wall with wood screws.

Her Reach-In Closet

A woman's closet is unique in several ways. This organizer features a full-length hanging space for dresses and coats, an area for folded items, and ample drawer space. In most cases, the hanging space will not have to be exceptionally high, so there will be more room for adequate shelf space above. The design in this project will work in a closet as narrow as 6 feet. For closets that are less than 6 feet wide, eliminate the shelf and drawer system. For very wide closets (10 feet or more) consider developing a more elaborate design.

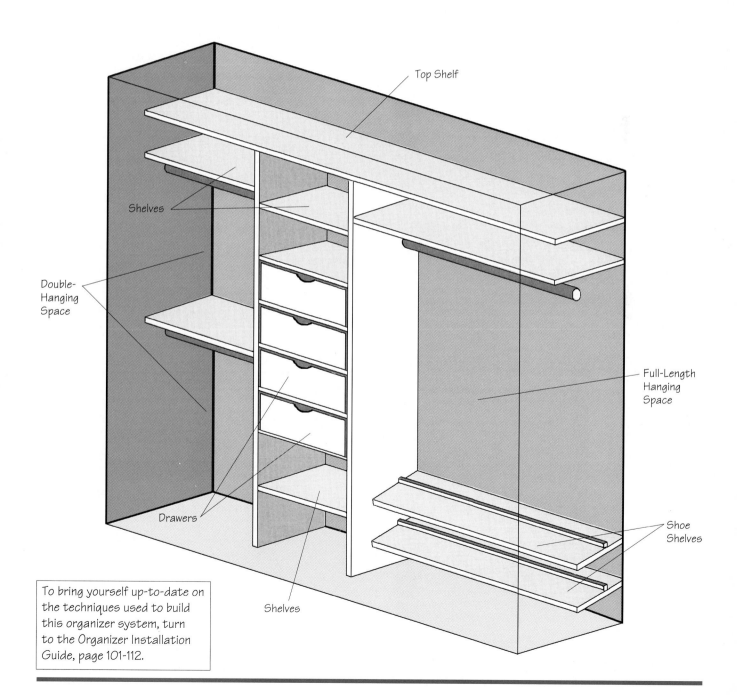

Top Shelf

Shelves

Double-Hanging Space

Drawers

Shelves

Full-Length Hanging Space

Shoe Shelves

To bring yourself up-to-date on the techniques used to build this organizer system, turn to the Organizer Installation Guide, page 101-112.

Hand-Built Organizer

Time Required:	Novice	Average	Experienced
	18 Hrs.	12 Hrs.	6 Hrs.

Tools & Materials

☐ Variable Speed Drill with Screwdriver Bit or Screwdriver
☐ Hammer
☐ Combination Square
☐ Pencil
☐ Table Saw (Optional)
☐ Circular Saw
☐ Miter Saw
☐ 1x4 (If needed at back wall)
☐ Paint or Stain
☐ 4d Finishing Nails
☐ Carpenter's Glue
☐ Router or Dado-Cutting Blade for Table Saw (For drawers)
☐ (2 or 3) Sheets 3/4" Plywood (Cut into 3 strips, 16" wide)
☐ (1/2) Sheet 1/4" Plywood (For drawers)
☐ 1x2 Furring - 1x1 or 45-degree Trim May Be Used (As needed)
☐ (12') 1x4 - Clear Grade or Number 1 Grade Fir or Pine
☐ 1x1 or Smaller Stock For Heel Stop (Optional)

☐ Measuring Tape
☐ Framing Square
☐ Utility Knife
☐ Jig Saw (For drawers)
☐ Level
☐ Crosscut (Hand) Saw
☐ Hanging Rod (As needed)
☐ 1¼" Wood Screws
☐ 2d Finishing Nails

NOTES: *1) The number of sheets of 3/4" plywood will depend on the width of the closet. 2) If the organizer is not going to be painted the same color as the closet, it is suggested that you sand first, then paint or stain the material before installing, and touch up afterward.*

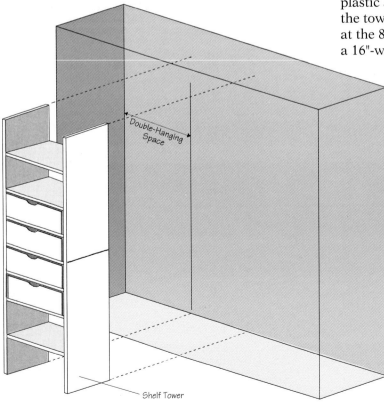

Install Shelf Tower

1 Select & Cut Plywood

The first step in building the organizer is to obtain the wood for the project. A guide to selecting and cutting plywood is found on page 101.

2 Build & Install Shelf Tower

Cut two strips of plywood 83¼" long. Determine the shelf arrangement you want, then multiply the number of shelves by two and cut as many 12"-long 1x2 furring strips. (You can also use 1x1 or 45-degree trim for the furring strips.) Cut the shelves to 1½" less than the desired width of the shelf tower. The design for this project shows a 22"-wide shelf tower, which means the shelves will be cut to 20½" wide. Determine the width of the shelf tower based on the width of the closet and the amount of items to be stored on shelves. Construct the shelf tower as detailed on pages 102-105.

Use the chart found on this page to determine the width of the double-hanging space on the left of the shelf tower, or set a dimension to meet your own preference and needs. Measure this distance from the left side of the closet and place a mark on the back wall of the closet. Use a level to draw a plumb, vertical line through the mark. As detailed on page 105, add two furrings strips to the back of the tower, at the top and bottom, and secure to the wall with plastic anchors and wood screws. Before securing the tower, however, measure the width of the closet at the 87" height and cut a shelf to that length from a 16"-wide strip of plywood. Set the shelf in place but do not secure, then secure the shelf tower. This is necessary because the top shelf may be difficult or impossible to install after the shelf tower is secure.

If the closet is more than 8' wide, the top shelf will have to be installed in two pieces. First, secure a 1x2 furring strip to the top of the right side of the shelf tower with wood screws. The seam in the top shelf should be directly above the seam between the right side of the shelf tower and the 1x2 furring strip. This should be done after the shelf tower is secured to the back wall of the closet. Do not secure the top shelf at this time.

Closet Width	Width of Double-Hanging Space
6'-7'	24"
7'-9'	30"
9'-10'	36"

3 *Install Rod & Shelf Supports*

Measure up 77¼" from the floor on the right side of the shelf tower. Use a level to draw a line along the right side of the tower at the mark. Continue the line along the back wall of the closet and wrap it around the right side wall. Use the level again to extend the line of the top of the shelf tower around the back wall and onto the right side wall.

On the left side of the closet draw another line from the top of the shelf tower around to the left side wall. Then draw lines at 41¼" and 77¼" above the floor. Be sure that all lines are level.

Construct three pairs of rod and shelf supports as detailed on page 101. Each pair should have a 16"-long support and a support as long as the closet is deep. Install two pairs on the left side of the closet at the two lower level lines. On the right side, install the third pair of rod and shelf supports at the lower level line.

Install 1x2 furring strips at the top lines on both sides. The furring strips are only needed on the side wall of the closet. They are not needed on the shelf tower unless the top shelf is being installed in two pieces as discussed above. If the hanging space on the right side is wider than 4', install a 1x4 on the back wall at the two lower level lines and a 1x2 at the upper level line.

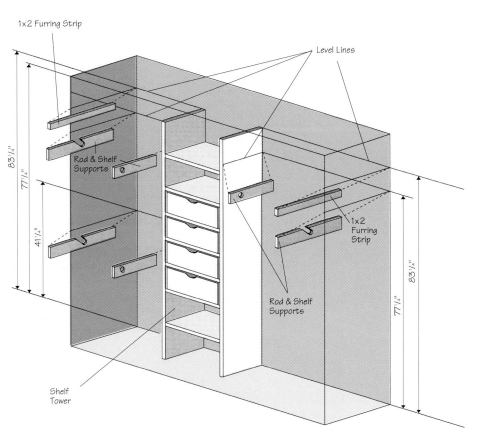

Install Rod & Shelf Supports

4 *Install Rods*

Measure the distance from the left side wall to the shelf tower at the lower pair of rod and shelf supports. Cut a length of rod to fit and insert one end into the support with the drilled hole only. Slide the other end into the slot cut in the opposite support. Repeat for all other rods.

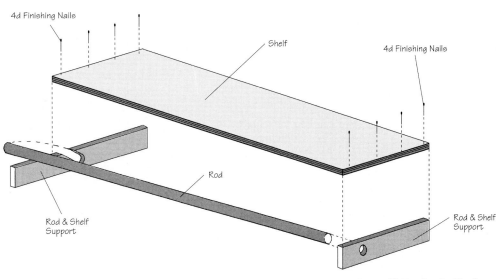

Install Rods & Shelves

5 *Install Shelves*

Turn to pages 102 for details on installing the shelves above the rods.

6 *Install Shoe Shelves*

Turn to page 107 for details on building and installing wooden, hand-built shoe shelves.

7 *Attach Trim Strips to Plywood*

Turn to page 103 for details on trimming the plywood.

Laminate Organizer

Time Required:	Novice 6 Hrs.	Average 4 Hrs.	Experienced 2 Hrs.

Tools & Materials (May vary depending on manufacturer.)

☐ Variable Speed Drill with Screwdriver Bit or Screwdriver

☐ Hammer	☐ Measuring Tape
☐ Pencil	☐ Level
☐ (1 or 2) Shelf Towers	☐ (3) Adjustable Rods
☐ Shoe Shelves	☐ (4) Shelves (Additional shelf optional)
☐ Shelf Tower	

Additional Items Needed (If not included in the shelf tower kit):

☐ (2) Angle Brackets	☐ (4) Plastic Anchors
☐ (4) 1" Wood Screws	☐ (4) 3/4" Wood Screws

NOTE: *Instructions for the installation of laminated systems are manufacturer specific. Only general instructions are given here.*

1 *Install Shelf Tower*

The shelf tower in this project has a combination of shelves and drawers. For details on laminated shelf towers, turn to page 108. The drawers are set in the middle of the tower for easier access. Use the chart (above right) to determine the width of the double-hanging space on the left of the shelf tower, or set a dimension that meets your own preference and needs. Measure this distance from the left side of the closet and place a mark on the back wall. Use a level to draw a vertical line at the mark. Assemble the shelf tower using the manufacturer's instructions and set it into place using the line you drew on the left side as a guide. Secure the tower to the back wall according to manufacturer's instructions or secure it with two angle brackets as detailed on page 108.

Closet Width	Width of Double- Hanging Space
6'-7'	24"
7'-9'	30"
9'-10'	36"

2 *Install Rods*

To install adjustable hanging rods, follow procedures described on page 20.

3 *Install Shelves*

A shelf above the rod on the right and above the top rod on the left will provide additional space for folded clothing, hats and other items. Determine the exact shelf arrangement, measure the length of the shelves, then cut and install per the manufacturer's instructions (see illustration page 23).

4 *Install Shoe Shelves*

Install the laminate shoe shelves according to the directions on page 108. (See illustration page 23 for placement).

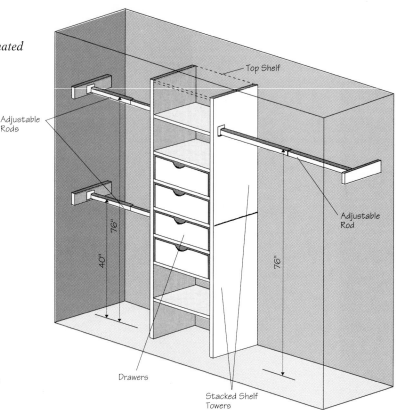

Top Shelf

Adjustable Rods

Adjustable Rod

76"

40"

76"

Drawers

Stacked Shelf Towers

Install Shelf Tower & Rods

Coated-Wire Organizer

Time Required:	Novice 5 Hrs.	Average 3 Hrs.	Experienced 1.5 Hrs.

Tools & Materials

- ☐ Variable Speed Drill with Screwdriver Bit or Screwdriver
- ☐ Hammer
- ☐ Measuring Tape
- ☐ Bolt Cutters or Hacksaw
- ☐ 12" Rod and Shelf (As needed)
- ☐ (1) 10-Runner Side Frame Set
- ☐ Wire-Basket Drawers
- ☐ (1) Set Leg Extensions (Optional)
- ☐ (1) Drawer System Top (Optional)
- ☐ (2) Sets Shoe Shelf Supports
- ☐ Down Clips
- ☐ Plastic Anchors
- ☐ 16" Rod and Shelf (As needed)
- ☐ 12" Organizer Shelf (As needed)
- ☐ (1) Set Floor Protectors (If not using casters)
- ☐ 12" Support Braces (As needed)
- ☐ Joiner Plate Assemblies (As needed)
- ☐ Pencil
- ☐ Level
- ☐ (30) Small End Caps
- ☐ (12) Large End Caps
- ☐ (1) Cross Brace Set
- ☐ Drawer Stops (As needed)
- ☐ (1) Set Casters (Optional)
- ☐ (5) End Brackets
- ☐ Back Clips
- ☐ Screws
- ☐ Hooks

1 *Install Back Clips*

Turn to pages 109-110, for a detailed look at a variety of clips and their installation.

Measure 42", 78" and 87" (adjust to the height of the user) up from the floor at the left corner of the closet and place marks on the back wall. At the 42" and 78" marks use a level to draw a horizontal line along the back wall. Use the following chart to determine the length of the line.

Closet Width	Bottom/Middle Shelf Lengths	Drawer System Width*
6'-7'	24"	17"
7'-8'	30"	17"
8'-9'	30"	22"
9'-10'	36"	22"

* Widths may vary depending upon manufacturer.

Use the level again to draw a horizontal line all the way across the closet back wall at the top mark.

Starting with any of the three lines, make a mark at 5/8" above the line and 2½" from the left side. Continue making marks 5/8" above the line and 12" apart until you reach the opposite end of the shelf line (2½" from the right side wall for the top line). Complete this procedure for all three lines. Install a back clip at each of the marks for hollow or masonry walls. For wood walls at least 1" thick, use down clips.

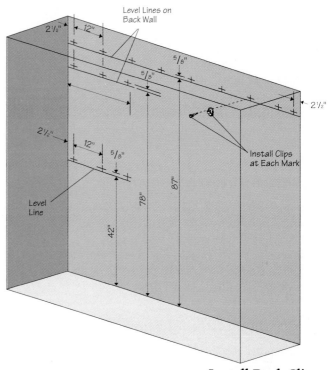

Install Back Clips

2 *Install Rods & Shelves*

The procedures for installing the top shelf are identical to those in Step 2 on page 21. Follow those directions and then return to this page to finish the step.

At the middle line cut a 16" integral rod and shelf to the selected length less 3/4". For the bottom line cut

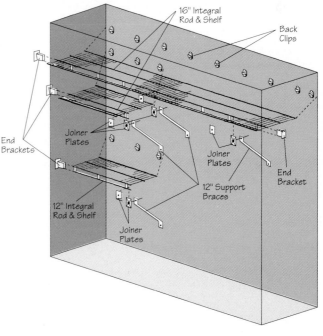

Install Rods & Shelves

a 12" integral rod and shelf to the selected length less 3/4". Slide end caps onto the cut ends of the wires of both shelves. Again, the two steel wires that make up the clothes hanging part of each shelf require large end caps. Snap the shelves into place as before. Install an end bracket at the left side wall and a 12" support brace at the right end of the shelf for both shelves (see page 110). For any shelf longer than $3\frac{1}{2}'$ add a support brace every $3\frac{1}{2}'$.

3 Install Drawer System

This design shows a 22"-wide wire-basket drawer system. If your closet is not as wide, however, you may prefer to use a 17"-wide system. Assemble the wire-basket drawer systems as detailed on page 112. Set in place at the end of the lower rod and shelf as shown.

4 Create Additional Storage

The area directly above the drawer system is shown as additional hanging space in the suggested design. You also can add a shelf or two using 12" or 16" organizer shelves with a support brace at each end, or you can stack an additional drawer system on top of the first.

If you are going to stack drawer systems, buy two 7-runner systems or a 10-runner and a 4-runner system. Do not exceed 14 runners. The drawers would be too high to reach. Build one frame without the top cross braces, then tap the L connectors in the bottom of a second frame into the top of the first frame. Slide the stacked drawer system into place in the closet. Do NOT put casters on a stacked

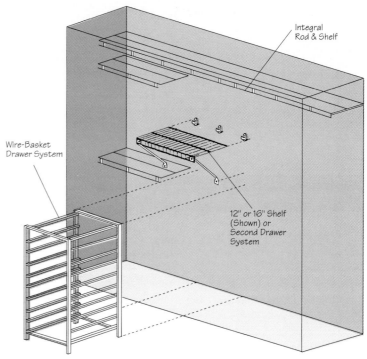

Install Drawer System

drawer system. While it will rest in the closet without any problems, two units high is not stable enough to be mobile.

5 Install Shoe Shelves

Two long shoe shelves are included in this system. At about 1' above the floor, measure the distance from the drawer system to the right side wall.

Cut two pieces of 12" organizer shelf to the measured length less $1\frac{1}{2}"$. (The additional amount subtracted is to allow ample clearance for the drawer system.) Set one shelf on the floor against the right side wall with the lip down and facing away from the back wall. Draw a line along the top and mark clip locations at $2\frac{1}{2}"$ from each end and every 12" between. Remove the shelf and install the back clips. Install a pair of shoe shelf supports on the shelf, then snap the shelf, lip up, into the clips. Lower it into position with the supports resting against the wall surface.

Set the second shelf on top of the first with the lip down and facing away from the back wall. Again, draw a line along the top and mark the clip locations. Install the second shelf in the same manner as the first. For more details on installing coated-wire shoe shelves, see page 111.

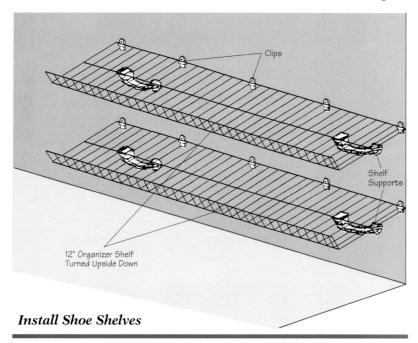

Install Shoe Shelves

His & Her Reach-In Closet

Some of the greatest marital arguments in history began over a shared closet, simply because nowhere is the difference between two people more noticeable. But sharing a closet does not have to mean risking a divorce. With careful organization, a shared reach-in closet will seem like two separate closets.

This design requires a closet of at least 9 feet in width. For narrower closets, eliminate one or both of the shelf towers.

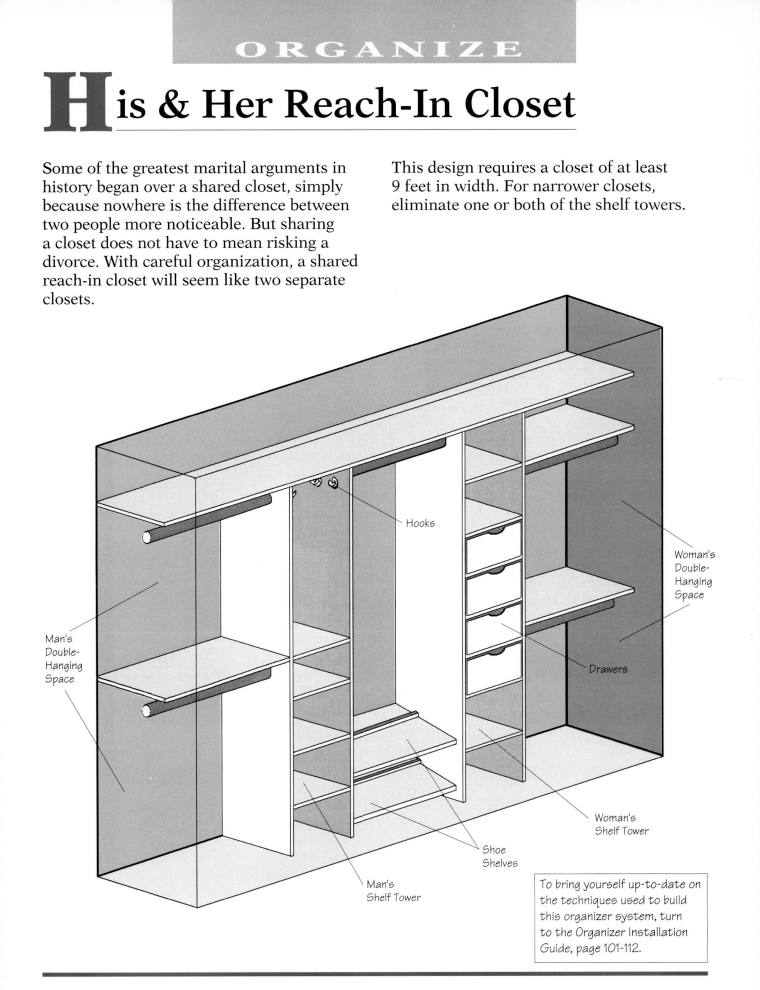

Hooks

Woman's Double-Hanging Space

Man's Double-Hanging Space

Drawers

Woman's Shelf Tower

Shoe Shelves

Man's Shelf Tower

To bring yourself up-to-date on the techniques used to build this organizer system, turn to the Organizer Installation Guide, page 101-112.

Hand-Built Organizers

Time Required:	Novice	Average	Experienced
	24 Hrs.	16 Hrs.	8 Hrs.

Tools & Materials

☐ Variable Speed Drill with Screwdriver Bit or Screwdriver

☐ Hammer   ☐ Measuring Tape

☐ Combination Square   ☐ Framing Square

☐ Pencil   ☐ Utility Knife

☐ Table Saw (Optional)   ☐ Jig Saw (For drawers)

☐ Circular Saw   ☐ Level

☐ Miter Saw   ☐ Crosscut (Hand) Saw

☐ 1x4 at Back Wall (If needed)   ☐ Hanging Rod (As needed)

☐ Paint or Stain   ☐ 1¼" Wood Screws

☐ 4d Finishing Nails   ☐ 2d Finishing Nails

☐ Carpenter's Glue

☐ Router or Dado-Cutting Blade for Table Saw (For drawers)

☐ (3) Sheets 3/4" Plywood (Cut into 3 strips, 16" wide)

☐ (1/2) Sheet 1/4" Plywood (For drawers)

☐ 1x2 Furring - 1x1 or 45-degree Trim May Be Used (As needed)

☐ (20') 1x4 - Clear Grade or Number 1 Grade

☐ 1x1 or Smaller Stock for Heel Stop (Optional)

NOTE: *1) The number of sheets of 3/4" plywood needed will depend on the width of the closet. 2) If the organizer is not going to be painted the same color as the closet, it is suggested that you sand first, then paint or stain the material before installing, and touch up afterward. This will be much easier than trying to paint precise lines where the organizer meets the closet walls.*

1 Select & Cut Plywood

The first step in building the organizer is to obtain the wood for the project. A guide to selecting and cutting plywood is found on page 101.

2 Build & Install Shelf Towers

Cut two strips of plywood to 83¼" long. Determine the shelf arrangement you want, then multiply the number of shelves by two and cut as many 12" long 1x2 furring strips. (You also can use 1x1 or 45-degree trim for the furring strips.) Cut the shelves to 1½" less than the desired width of the shelf tower. The design for this project has a 15"-wide shelf tower, which means the shelves will be cut to 13½" wide. Determine the width of your shelf tower based on closet width and the amount of items to be stored on shelves. Construct the shelf tower as shown on pages 102-106. Repeat the process for the second shelf tower.

Whatever width towers you use, subtract the combined widths from the measured width of the closet. Divide the remainder by three to get the width of each of the three hanging areas. Carefully survey the clothes to be hung. Use the dimensions presented in the charts on page 10, to adjust these widths as necessary.

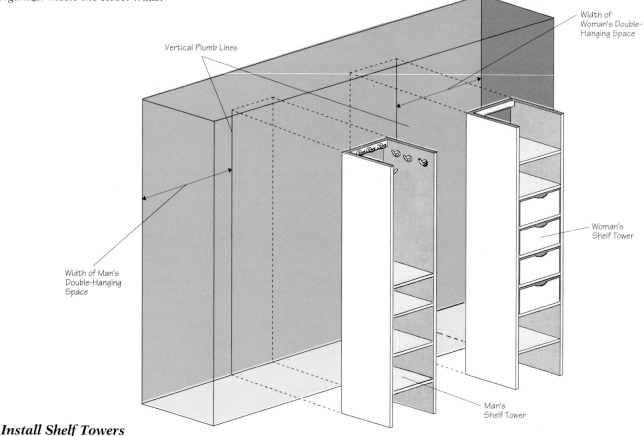

Width of Woman's Double-Hanging Space

Vertical Plumb Lines

Woman's Shelf Tower

Width of Man's Double-Hanging Space

Man's Shelf Tower

Install Shelf Towers

Measure the predetermined width for the woman's double-hanging area from the right side of the closet and place a mark on the back wall of the closet. Use a level to draw a plumb, vertical line through the mark. As detailed on page 105, add two furring strips to the back of the tower, at the top and bottom and secure to the wall with plastic anchors and wood screws.

For closets less than 8' wide, the top shelf should be set in place before securing the shelf tower(s). Measure the width of the closet at the 84" height and cut a shelf to that length from a 16"-wide strip of plywood. Set the shelf in place but do not secure, then secure the shelf tower. This is necessary because the top shelf may be difficult or impossible to install after the shelf tower is secure.

If the closet is more than 8' wide, the top shelf will have to be installed in two pieces. The seam in the top shelf should be directly above the seam between the right side of the man's shelf tower and the rod and shelf support. This should be done after the shelf tower is secured to the closet back wall. Do not secure the top shelf at this time.

3 Install Rod & Shelf Supports

Measure up 35¼" and 71¼" from the floor on the right side of the woman's shelf tower. Use a level to draw two level lines along the right side of the tower at the marks. Continue the level lines along the back wall of the closet and wrap around onto the right side wall. Use the level again to extend the line of the top of the shelf tower around the back wall and onto the right side wall.

On the left side of the closet draw level lines from the top of the shelf tower around to the left side wall. Then draw a level line at 44¼" above the floor.

Construct five pairs of rod and shelf supports as detailed on page 101. Four of the pairs should have a 16"-long support and a support as long as the closet is deep. For the center pair, both pieces should be 16" long. Install two pairs on the right side of the closet at the two lower level lines. Install two more pairs at the level lines on the left side. Install the center pair at the tops of the shelf towers.

Install a 1x2 furring strip at the top line on the right side wall of the closet. This is to support the top shelf. If any of the three hanging spaces are wider than 4 feet, install a 1x4 on the back wall at the appropriate lower level line.

4 Install Rods

To install the adjustable rods, follow instructions found on page 25.

5 Install Shelves

Turn to page 102 for instructions on installing shelves above the rods. Install the top shelf last.

6 Install Shoe Shelves

Turn to page 107 for details on building and installing wooden, hand-built shoe shelves (see illustration page 29 for placement of shoe shelves).

7 Attach Trim Strips to Shelves

Turn to page 103 for details on trimming the plywood.

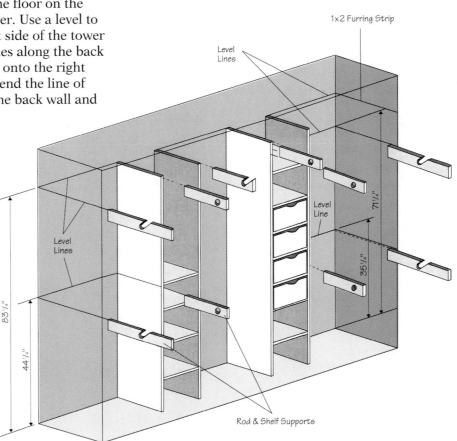

Install Rods & Shelves

Laminate Organizer

Time Required:	Novice	Average	Experienced
	9 Hrs.	6 Hrs.	3 Hrs.

Tools & Materials (May vary according to manufacturer.)

☐ Variable Speed Drill with Screwdriver Bit or Screwdriver

☐ Hammer   ☐ Measuring Tape

☐ Pencil   ☐ Level

☐ (2 or 4) Shelf Towers   ☐ (5) Adjustable Rods

☐ Shelf Tower   ☐ Shoe Shelves

☐ (4) Shelves (2 Additional shelves optional)

Additional Items Needed to Secure Shelf Towers to Wall (If the hardware is not included in the shelf tower kits):

☐ (4) Angle Brackets   ☐ (8) Plastic Anchors

☐ (8) 1" Wood Screws   ☐ (8) 3/4" Wood Screws

NOTE: *Instructions for the installation of laminated systems are manufacturer specific. Only general instructions are given here.*

1 Install Shelf Towers

This project provides a combination of shelves, drawers and hanging hooks within two 15"-wide towers. The man's shelf tower features hooks at the top while the woman's tower has drawers in the middle area.

For details on laminated shelf towers, turn to page 108.

Whatever width towers you use, subtract the combined widths from the measured width of the closet. Divide the remainder by three to get the width of each of the three hanging areas. Carefully survey the clothes to be hung. Use the chart on page 10 to adjust these widths as necessary.

Measure the predetermined width for the man's double-hanging area from the left side of the closet and place a mark on the back wall. Use a level to draw a vertical line at the mark. Assemble the man's shelf tower per the manufacturer's directions and set in place in the closet with the left side on the line drawn on the back wall.

Secure the tower to the back wall following the manufacturer's directions, if provided. If not, secure with two angle brackets as detailed on page 108.

Measure the predetermined width of the woman's double-hanging area from the right side of the closet and draw another vertical line. Install the woman's shelf tower in the same manner.

2 Install Rods

Measure the length needed for each of the five rods in this design and buy adjustable rods accordingly (see page 108). Install per the manufacturer's directions 43" and 82" above the floor on the left side of the closet, 82" above the floor in the center, and 34" and 70" above the floor on the right side of the closet. Use a level when installing the rods. The distance from the closet back wall to the rod is based on the depth of the closet as shown in the following chart.

Closet Depth	Dimension
23" or More	12"
20" to 23"	1/2 Closet Depth
20" or Less	10"

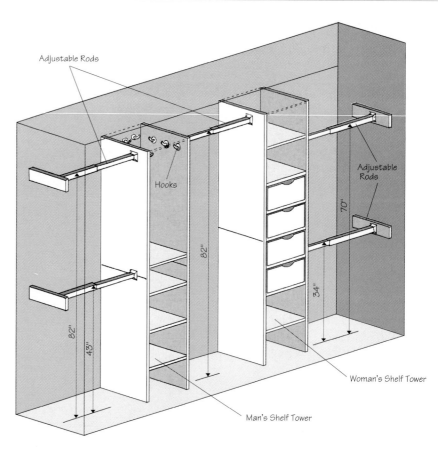

Install Shelf Towers & Rods

3 Install Shelves

A shelf above the top three rods and an additional shelf at the 84" mark on the right side provides additional space for folding clothes, hats and other items. Determine the exact shelf arrangement, measure the length of the shelves, then cut and install per the manufacturer's directions (see illustration page 29 for placement).

4 Install Shoe Shelves

Install the laminate shoe shelves according to the directions found on page 108. (See illustration page 29 for placement).

Coated-Wire Organizer

Time Required:	Novice 6 Hrs.	Average 4 Hrs.	Experienced 2 Hrs.

Tools & Materials

☐ Variable Speed Drill with Screwdriver Bit or Screwdriver
☐ Hammer
☐ Measuring Tape
☐ 12" Rod and Shelf (As needed)
☐ 12" Organizer Shelf (As needed)
☐ 16 Large End Caps
☐ (3) Cross Brace Sets
☐ Drawer Stops (As needed)
☐ Back Clips
☐ (2) Sets Shoe Shelf Supports
☐ Plastic Anchors
☐ (2) Sets Floor Protectors (If not using casters)
☐ (2) Sets Leg Extensions (Optional)
☐ (2) Sets Casters (Optional)
☐ 12" Support Braces (As needed)
☐ Bolt Cutters or Hacksaw
☐ (2) Drawer-System Tops (Optional)
☐ Joiner Plate Assemblies (As needed)

☐ Pencil
☐ Level
☐ 16" Rod and Shelf (As needed)
☐ (36) Small End Caps
☐ (3) 7-Runner Side Frame Sets
☐ Wire-Basket Drawers
☐ (5) End Brackets
☐ Screws
☐ Down Clips
☐ Hooks

1 Install Back Clips

Turn to pages 109-110 for a detailed look at a variety of clips and their installation.

For closets under 12' wide use 17" drawer systems. For wider closets, use 22" drawer systems. Measure the width of the closet and subtract the total width of the two drawer systems. Divide the remainder by three to get the width of each of the three hanging areas. Carefully survey the clothes to be hung. Use the dimensions presented in the charts on page 10 to adjust these widths as necessary.

Measure 45" and 84" (adjust for the height of the user) up from the floor at the left corner of the closet and place marks on the back wall. At the 45" mark use a level to draw a horizontal line along the back wall. The line should be as long as the predetermined width of the man's double-hanging area. At the 84" mark draw a horizontal line across the back wall of the closet from side wall to side wall.

Measure 36" and 72" (adjust for the height of the female user) up from the floor in the right corner of the closet and place marks on the back wall. At each mark use a level to draw a horizontal line across the back wall. Both lines should be as long as the predetermined width of the woman's double-hanging area. For tall women, raise the lower shelf and use the 84" line for the second shelf, eliminating one of the shelves above the double-hanging area.

Starting with the left side of the top line, make a mark at 5/8" above the line and 2½" from the left side. Continue making marks 5/8" above the line and 12" apart until you reach the right side wall. Make a final mark at 2½" from the right side wall. Repeat the procedure for the line at the 45" height, except that the last mark is at the end of the line. Repeat again for the two lines on the right side of the closet. For hollow or masonry walls, install a back clip at each of the marks. For wood walls at least 1" thick, use down clips.

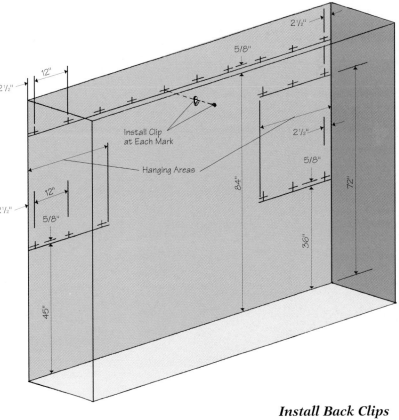

Install Back Clips

2 Install Rods & Shelves

The procedure for installing the top shelf is identical to that in Step 2, on page 21. Follow those directions and then return to this page.

At the 72" line in the woman's double-hanging area, cut 16" integral rod and shelf to the selected length less 3/4". For the lower lines in both the man's and woman's double-hanging areas cut 12" integral rod and shelf to the selected lengths less 3/4". Slide end caps onto the cut ends of the wires of both shelves. Again, the two steel wires that make up the clothes hanging part of each shelf require large end caps. Snap the shelves into place as before. Install an end bracket at the side wall and a 12" support brace at the open end of each of the three shorter shelves (see page 110). For shelves longer than 3½', install an additional support brace every 3½'.

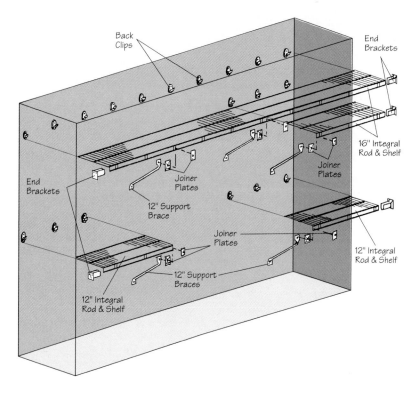

Install Rods & Shelves

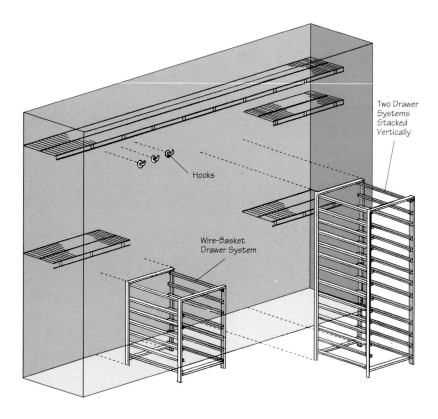

Install Drawer Systems

3 Install Drawer Systems

Assemble the wire-basket drawer systems as detailed on page 112. Set in place as shown left.

4 Additional Storage

The woman's shelf tower utilizes two 7-runner drawer systems stacked vertically (see Step 4 on page 28 for ways to get additional storage).

5 Install Shoe Shelves

Two shoe shelves are included in the center of the closet, at the bottom of the shared full-length hanging area. Measure the distance between the drawer systems. For installation, follow the procedures found on page 111 (see illustration page 29 for placement.)

Child's Reach-In Closet

Scaling a closet to a child's size encourages independence by making it possible for him or her to reach clothing and objects without assistance. Place the lower rod within easy reach and keep out-of-season clothing on an upper rod or shelf. Leave enough space between hanging rods for growing room. The design in this project will work in a closet that is 5 feet wide. For closets that are less wide, eliminate a portion of the shelf system. For extra wide closets (9 feet or more) consider developing a more elaborate design.

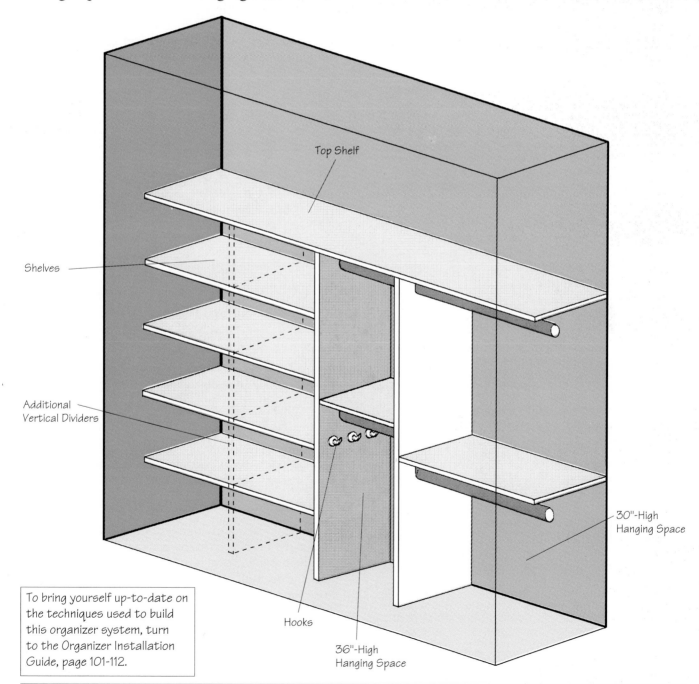

Top Shelf

Shelves

Additional
Vertical Dividers

30"-High
Hanging Space

Hooks

36"-High
Hanging Space

To bring yourself up-to-date on the techniques used to build this organizer system, turn to the Organizer Installation Guide, page 101-112.

Hand-Built Organizer

Time Required:	Novice 18 Hrs.	Average 12 Hrs.	Experienced 6 Hrs.

Tools & Materials

☐ Variable Speed Drill with Screwdriver Bit or Screwdriver
☐ Drill Bits
☐ Measuring Tape
☐ Framing Square
☐ Utility Knife
☐ Circular Saw
☐ Miter Saw
☐ 1x4 (If needed at back wall)
☐ Paint or Stain (As desired)
☐ 1 1/4" Wood Screws
☐ Plastic Anchors
☐ 2d Finishing Nails
☐ Sandpaper
☐ Hammer
☐ Combination Square
☐ Pencil
☐ Table Saw (Optional)
☐ Level
☐ Crosscut (Hand) Saw
☐ Hanging Rod (As needed)
☐ 3/4" Screen Mold
☐ 1 3/4" Wood Screws
☐ 4d Finishing Nails
☐ Carpenter's Glue
☐ (2 or 3) Sheets 3/4" Plywood (Cut into 3 strips, 16" wide)
☐ 1x2 Furring - 1x1 or 45-degree Trim May Be Used (As needed)
☐ (12') 1x4-Clear Grade or Number 1 Grade Fir or Pine

NOTE: *If the organizer is not going to be painted the same color as the closet, it is suggested that you sand first, then paint or stain the material before installing, and touch up afterward. This will be much easier than trying to paint precise lines where the organizer meets the closet walls.*

1 Select & Cut Plywood

The first step in building the organizer is to obtain the wood for the project. A guide to selecting and cutting plywood is found on page 101.

2 Install Right Vertical Divider & Shelf

Measure the width of the closet at the 66" height and cut a 16"-wide strip of plywood to that length if less than 8'. This is the top shelf. If the closet is wider than 8', the shelf will have to be pieced. Cut only to the length necessary to span the shelf area and the 36" hanging area. Use the chart below to determine the distance that suits your needs.

Closet Width Chart

Closet Width	Width of Lower 30" Hanging Area	Width of Hook 36" Hanging Area	Width of Shelf Area
5'	2'	1'	2'
6'	2' 6"	1'	2' 6"
7'	2' 6"	1' 6"	3'
8'	3'	1' 6"	3' 6"
9'	3' 6"	2'	3' 6"

Measure 65¼" from the floor in the back left corner of the closet and make a mark. Use a level to draw a horizontal line all the way across the back wall of the closet. Extend the line onto both side walls. Install a 1x2 furring strip at the line on the left side wall. Measure over the distance of the 30" hanging area from the right side wall. Use a level to draw a plumb vertical line at the mark. Measure the distance from the floor to the horizontal line on the back wall and cut a strip of 16"-wide plywood to that length. This is the right vertical divider between the 30" and 36" hanging areas. Have one person hold the right vertical divider in place on the vertical line while the top shelf is set in place. Nail the top shelf to the 1x2 furring strip and the vertical divider with one 4d finishing nail each. Do not drive the nail all the way into the wood. It is temporary and will be removed later. If the top shelf extends to the right side wall, that end will be secured later.

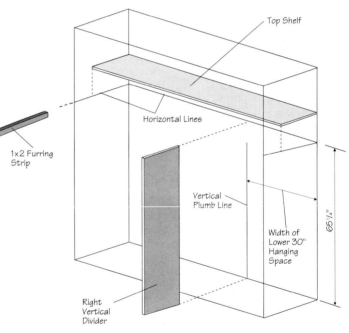

Top Shelf

Horizontal Lines

1x2 Furring Strip

Vertical Plumb Line

Width of Lower 30" Hanging Space

65¼"

Right Vertical Divider

Install Right Vertical Divider & Shelf

3 Install Left Vertical Divider

Before the vertical dividers are installed, the shelf lines must be drawn on the back wall. The design for this project shows four shelves, though you can adjust if desired. Measure up 11¼", 24¾", 38¼" and 51¾" (or to 3/4" less than desired shelf heights) from the floor in the left corner of the closet. Draw a horizontal line at each mark along the left side wall and along the back wall to the desired width of the shelf area. Make sure the lines are level.

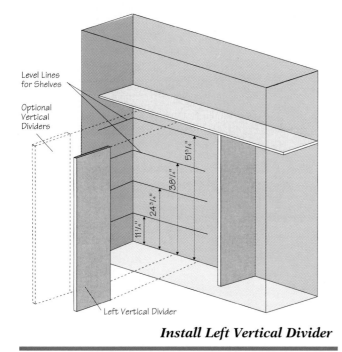

Install Left Vertical Divider

The shelf system shown spans the full width of the shelf area with a single vertical divider at the right end of the shelves. If you prefer, you can create "cubby holes" by adding vertical dividers. Cubby holes are good for storing toys. Determine the number and location of the vertical dividers, then measure from the floor to the shelf top at each location and cut a strip of 16"-wide plywood to fit. Set each in place and nail the top shelf to the dividers with one 4d finishing nail each. Again, these are temporary. Do not nail them all the way into the wood. Use a level to keep the dividers plumb. There is no need to secure them to the floor; gravity will take care of it.

4 Secure Vertical Dividers

Measure the distance between the vertical dividers at the top of the lower 36"-high hanging space. Cut a

1x2 furring strip to the measured distance. Hold the furring strip in place between the vertical dividers, just below the top shelf. Using a 1/8" drill bit, drill three holes through the strip, one at each end and one in the middle. Remove the furring strip and drill the three holes in the wall with a 1/4" bit. Insert a plastic anchor into each hole. Set the furring strip back into place and secure to the plastic anchors with 1¾" wood screws. Finally, secure each end of the furring strip to the vertical dividers with two 1¼" wood screws. Drill a pilot hole, then install the screws. Be sure the vertical dividers are flush against the back wall.

5 Install Shelves

Measure the depth of the closet on the left side and cut four 1x2 furring strips to the measured distance. (You also can use 1x1 or 45-degree trim for the furring strips.) Cut four more furring strips to 12" long. (If you installed additional vertical dividers, you will need eight 12" furring strips for each.) Secure the furring strips to the left side wall with the top of each strip on a level shelf line. Use a level to extend the lines 12" onto each vertical divider, then install the furring strips with three 1¼" wood screws per strip.

If the shelves span more than 4' before reaching a vertical divider, an additional 1x2 furring strip is needed at the level line on the back wall. Nail to the studs with 10d finishing nails.

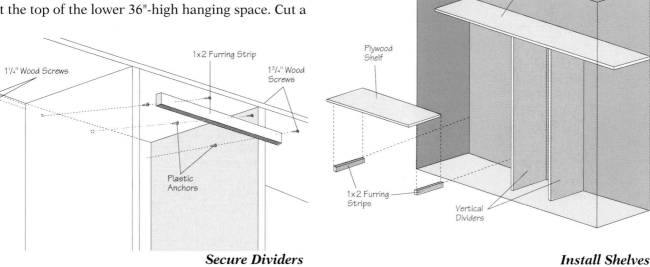

Secure Dividers

Install Shelves

6 *Install Rod & Shelf Support*

Measure up 29¼" from the floor in the back right corner of the closet. Use a level to draw a line along the right side wall and the back wall to the width of the lower 30" hanging area. Continue the line along the right side of the right vertical divider. Draw another level line at 35¼" from the floor, inside the lower 36" hanging area.

Construct four pairs of rod and shelf supports as detailed on page 101. Two pairs should have a 16"-long support and a support as long as the closet is deep at the right side wall. For the remaining two pairs, all four pieces should be 16" long. Install the four pairs of rod and shelf supports as shown. Measure the length necessary for the rod in the lower 30" hanging area. Cut a length of rod to fit and insert one end into the support with the drilled hole only. Slide the other end into the slot cut in the opposite support. Repeat for the lower 36" hanging area, then repeat for the upper hanging area. Remove the temporary nails in the top shelf and lift out of the way as necessary.

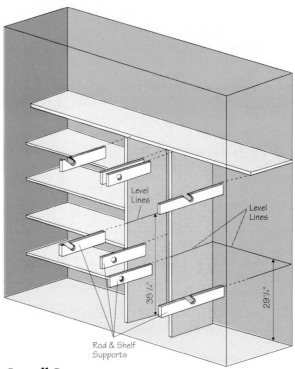

Install Supports

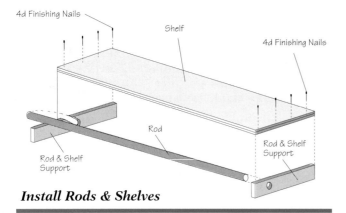

Install Rods & Shelves

7 *Install Shelves Above Hanging Rods*

Measure and cut the shelves above the lower hanging rods using 16"-wide plywood. If the plywood you are using is better on one side than the other, place the better side up. Secure with four 4d finishing nails at each end of each shelf. For longer shelves with a 1x4 support at the back wall, secure with 4d finishing nails every 12".

For the top shelf, use four 4d nails at each end and at every vertical divider. If the top shelf had to be installed in two pieces, measure the distance from the end of the first piece to the right side wall and cut a strip of 16"-wide plywood to fit. Set in place and nail into the two rod and shelf supports at each end with four 4d finishing nails.

8 *Attach Trim Strips to Plywood*

Turn to page 103 for details on trimming the shelves.

Laminate Organizer

Time Required:	Novice	Average	Experienced
	6 Hrs.	4 Hrs.	2 Hrs.

Tools & Materials (May vary according to manufacturer.)

☐ Variable Speed Drill with Screwdriver Bit or Screwdriver

☐ Hammer   ☐ Measuring Tape

☐ Pencil   ☐ Level

☐ Shelf Tower   ☐ (4) Adjustable Rods

☐ Shelves (Stackable or Permanent)

☐ Long Shelf for Top of Closet

Additional Items Needed (If not included in the shelf tower kit):

☐ (4) Angle Brackets   ☐ (8) Plastic Anchors

☐ (8) 1" Wood Screws   ☐ (8) 3/4" Wood Screws

NOTE: *Instructions for the installation of laminated systems are manufacturer specific. Only general instructions are given here.*

1 *Install Shelf Tower*

This project provides both a shelf tower and stackable shelves. For details on laminated shelf towers, turn to page 108. In the left corner there are four shelves stacked on top of each other. Just to the right of the shelves there is a shelf tower with two hanging rods. Hanging hooks, located on the bottom of the tower, are optional. The lower hanging space is for coats or a robe.

Measure over the proper width for the shelf area in the left side of the closet and make a mark on the back wall. Use the closet width chart (page 36) to determine the width of the shelf area, or set the width to meet your specific needs.

NOTE: *Most laminate systems contain adjustable rods that are a minimum of 18". If you are using a laminate organizer, consider using coated-wire integral rod and shelf for the hanging areas.*

Use a level to draw a plumb, vertical line through the mark. Assemble the shelf tower per the manufacturer's directions and set in place with the left side of the tower on the line drawn on the back wall. Secure to the back wall following the manufacturer's directions, if provided. If not, secure with two angle brackets as detailed on page 108.

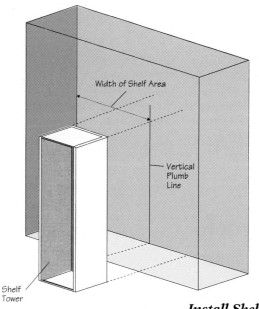

Install Shelf Tower

2 *Install Shelves*

For stackable shelves, place the units in the lower left part of the closet, between the left side wall and shelf tower. Follow the manufacturer's directions if you have chosen a different type of shelf. You also may install coated-wire or hand-built shelves with the laminate shelf tower.

3 *Install Rods & Hooks*

For details on rods, see page 20, Step 2. Then, finish this step with the procedures that follow.

Install an adjustable rod at 28" and 64" above the floor between the right side wall and the right side of the shelf tower. Follow the manufacturer's directions and use a level when installing the rod. The distance from the back wall of the closet to the rod is based on the depth of the closet as shown on page 20.

Install two additional rods inside the shelf tower, one at 34" and a second at 64". Install rods of the appropriate size adjusted to the required length at the two heights inside the shelf tower.

The installation of hooks is optional. In this design the area for hooks is in the lower 36" high hanging area (for details on hooks, see page 112).

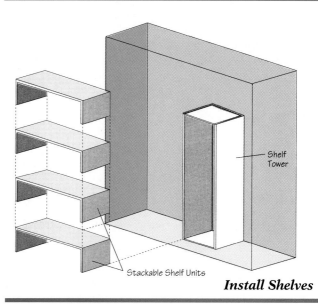

Install Shelves

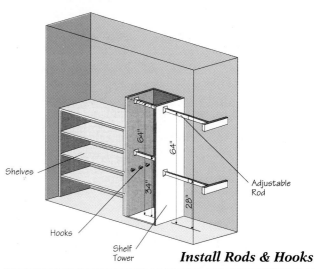

Install Rods & Hooks

4 *Install Top Shelf*

For storage of rarely used items, add a top shelf on either side of the tower. Purchase a laminate shelf of the necessary length and install per the manufacturer's directions. For larger closets the shelf may have to be installed in two pieces. The seam should be directly above one side of the shelf tower. You also can place a shelf over the lower rod on the right, though clothes may hang too low to use it for storage. An additional shelf can be added above the top shelf, but it will not be accessible to a small child.

Coated-Wire Organizer

Time Required:	Novice	Average	Experienced
	5 Hrs.	3 Hrs.	1.5 Hrs.

Tools & Materials

☐ Variable Speed Drill with Screwdriver Bit or Screwdriver
☐ Pencil   ☐ Measuring Tape
☐ Level   ☐ Bolt Cutters or Hacksaw
☐ 12" Rod and Shelf (As needed)   ☐ 16" Rod and Shelf (As needed)
☐ Small End Caps (As needed)   ☐ (12) Large End Caps
☐ 12" Support Braces (As needed) ☐ (6) End Brackets
☐ (1) Support Pole   ☐ Back Clips
☐ Down Clips   ☐ Screws
☐ Plastic Anchors   ☐ Hooks
☐ 12" or 16" Organizer Shelf (As needed)
☐ Joiner Plate Assemblies (As needed)

1 *Install Back Clips*

Turn to pages 109-110 for a detailed look at a variety of clips and their installation. Measure 30" and 66" (adjust for the height of the child, but allow room for growth) up from the floor at the right corner of the closet and place marks on the back wall. At the 30" mark use a level to draw a horizontal line along the back wall. Determine the length of the line from the closet width chart (page 36), or set to your own specifications based on the clothes and other items to be stored in the closet.

Measure up 36" at the end of the first line and draw another level line. The length of the line should be equal to the width of the 36" hanging area. Use the level again at the 66" mark, drawing a horizontal line from wall to wall.

Measure up 12", 25½", 39" and 52½" at the left side of the closet. Draw a level line at each of the four marks to the width of the shelf area. You can make the shelves closer together to suit your needs if you are using 12" shelving. If you use 16" shelving, however, it can be no closer than 13½" or there will be

interference from the support braces. If using an integral rod and shelf this is not a problem.

Starting with any line, make a mark at 5/8" above the line and 2½" from the side wall. Continue making marks 5/8" above the line and 12" apart until you reach the opposite end of the shelf line (2½" from the opposite wall for the full length line at the top). Complete this process for all seven lines. For hollow or masonry walls, install a back clip at each of the marks. For wood walls that are at least 1" thick, use down clips.

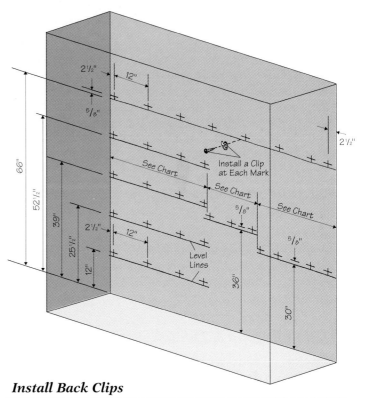

Install Back Clips

2 *Install Rods & Shelves*

The procedure for installing the top shelf is identical to that in Step 2, page 21. Follow those directions then return to this page.

At the 30" line on the right side, measure the length of the shelf and cut 12" integral rod and shelf to the measured length less 3/4". Slide end caps onto the cut ends of the wires. Again, the two steel wires that make up the clothes hanging part of the shelf require large end caps. Snap into place as before. Install an end bracket at the right side wall and a 12" support brace at the left end of the shelf. If the shelf is longer than 3½', install an additional support brace every 3½', starting from the side wall on the right (see page 110).

At the 36" line cut 12" integral rod and shelf to the measured length. Install with a 12" support brace on the right end. Leave the left end free until after the organizer shelves are installed.

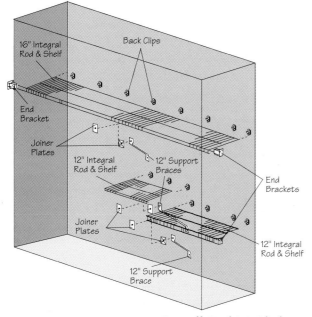

Install Rods & Shelves

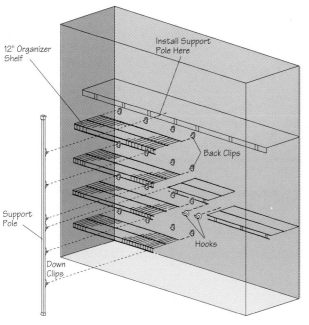

Install Support Pole & Hooks

3 *Install Organizer Shelves*

For the shelf area, measure the length of each shelf and cut 12" organizer shelf to 3/4" less than the measured lengths. You can use 16" organizer shelf if you prefer. (Although you can mix 12" and 16" organizer shelf, the open ends will have to be supported with support braces instead of a support pole.) Slide small end caps on the four cut wires at each end of the shelf (five cut wires each end for 16" shelving). Install with an end bracket at the left side wall. If the shelves are longer than 3½', use 12" or 16" support braces (depending on the shelf width) every 3½'.

4 *Install Support Pole*

Once all four organizer shelves are in place, install the support pole as detailed on page 111. The support pole is attached to the right side of all four organizer shelves and the left side of the 12" integral rod and shelf at the 36" line. It can be cut so that it falls below the 16" integral rod and shelf at the top of the closet, or you can slide through the shelf from the bottom and attach to the hanging part of the shelf.

If you used 16" organizer shelves the pole support should be attached to the four shelves and the outside wire of the 16" integral rod and shelf at the top. Install a 12" support brace on the left side of the 12" integral rod and shelf at the 36" line.

5 *Install Hooks*

The installation of hooks for playthings and a variety of children's items is optional. In this design the area for hooks is in the lower 36" high hanging area. This area also can be used for hanging clothes if preferred, particularly since the integral rod and shelf is already in place. For details on types of hanging hooks, turn to page 112.

His Walk-In Closet

A walk-in closet provides a large amount of storage space while keeping everything within easy reach. In a man's walk-in closet there is plenty of double-hanging space, along with ample shelf footage, shoe storage and a full-length hanging area. The design in this project is based on a typical 6-foot-wide by 7-foot-deep walk-in closet, but will work as well for larger closets. For much larger walk-ins consider a more elaborate design. For smaller walk-ins reduce the 36-inch dimension for the full-length and hook-hanging areas.

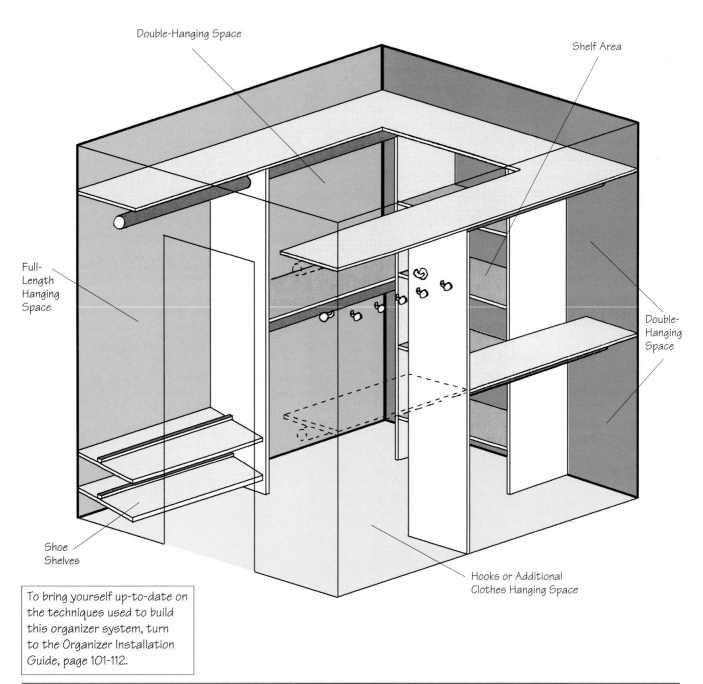

Double-Hanging Space

Shelf Area

Full-Length Hanging Space

Double-Hanging Space

Shoe Shelves

Hooks or Additional Clothes Hanging Space

To bring yourself up-to-date on the techniques used to build this organizer system, turn to the Organizer Installation Guide, page 101-112.

Hand-Built Organizer

Time Required:	Novice	Average	Experienced
	18 Hrs.	12 Hrs.	8 Hrs.

Tools & Materials

☐ Variable Speed Drill with Screwdriver Bit or Screwdriver

☐ Hammer

☐ Combination Square

☐ Pencil

☐ Table Saw (Optional)

☐ Level

☐ Crosscut (Hand) Saw

☐ 3/4" Screen Mold

☐ 1¼" Wood Screws

☐ 4d Finishing Nails

☐ Carpenter's Glue

☐ Measuring Tape

☐ Framing Square

☐ Utility Knife

☐ Circular Saw

☐ Miter Saw

☐ Hanging Rod (As needed)

☐ Paint or Stain

☐ 1³/₄" Wood Screws

☐ 2d Finishing Nails

☐ Sandpaper

☐ 1x1 or Smaller Stock for Heel Stop (Optional)

☐ (3) Sheets 3/4" Plywood (Cut into 3 Strips, 16" Wide)

☐ 1x2 Furring - 1x1 or 45-degree Trim May Be Used (As needed)

☐ 1x4 - Clear Grade or Number 1 Grade (As needed)

Additional Items Needed to Secure Each Vertical Divider to the Wall:

☐ (2) Angle Brackets

☐ (4) 1" Wood Screws

☐ (4) Plastic Anchors

☐ (4) 3/4" Wood Screws

NOTE: *If the organizer is not going to be painted the same color as the closet, it is suggested that you sand first, then paint or stain the material before installing, and touch up afterward. This will be much easier than trying to paint precise lines where the organizer meets the closet walls.*

1 Select & Cut Plywood

The first step in building the organizer is to obtain the wood. A guide to selecting and cutting plywood is found on page 101.

2 Install Side Wall Vertical Dividers

Measure 83¼" from the floor at the back wall and place a mark on the wall. Use a level to draw horizontal lines all along the back wall and both side walls. Extend the lines 16" onto the front wall at each side. Measure 36" from the front wall along each side wall and make a mark on the side wall. (Adjust the 36" dimension for smaller closets.)

Measure the distance from the floor to the line at the mark on each side wall and cut strips of 16" plywood to fit. These are the vertical dividers. Secure the vertical dividers to the walls in the same manner as explained for securing a laminated shelf tower on page 108.

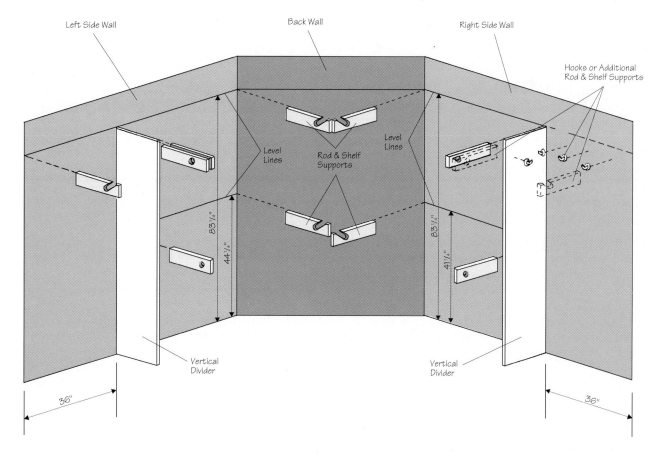

Install Vertical Dividers, Rod & Shelf Supports, Hooks

3 Install Rod & Shelf Supports

Measure 44¼" from the floor at the back left corner of the closet and 41¼" at the back right corner of the closet. Use a level to draw a line along the side walls at the marks. Continue the lines 16" along the back wall and along the side wall vertical dividers. Make sure all lines are level.

Construct five pairs of rod and shelf supports as detailed on page 101. For a walk-in closet, all rod and shelf supports should be 16" long. Install two pairs on the right side of the closet at the level lines as shown on the previous page. On the left side, install three pairs of rod and shelf supports. If you are installing a hanging rod rather than hooks on the right side wall, it will need supports as well (see illustration previous page).

4 Install Hooks

Install the hooks as detailed page 112 (see illustration previous page for placement).

5 Build & Install Shelf Tower

Cut two strips of plywood to 83¼" long. Determine the shelf arrangement you want, then multiply the number of shelves by two and cut as many 12"-long 1x2 furring strips. (You can also use 1x1 or 45-degree trim for the furring strips.) This project has five shelves which would require 10 furring strips.

For a 6'-wide closet, we suggest that you use a 24" shelf tower. The shelf tower should be a minimum of 22"—preferably more—from each side wall. Cut the shelves to 1½" less than the desired width of the shelf tower. The design for this project shows a 24"-wide shelf tower, which means the shelves will be cut to 22½" wide. Construct the shelf tower as detailed on pages 102-104. Install the bottom shelf first and work up one shelf at a time.

Determine the distance from the side wall to the side of the shelf tower. Measure that distance from either side wall and place a mark on the back wall. Use a level to draw a plumb, vertical line through the mark. As detailed on page 105, add two furring strips to the back of the tower, at the top and bottom, and secure to the wall with plastic anchors and 1¾" wood screws.

6 Install Rods

Measure the distance from the vertical divider to the back wall at the upper pair of rod and shelf supports on the left side wall. Cut a length of rod to fit and insert one end into the support with the drilled hole

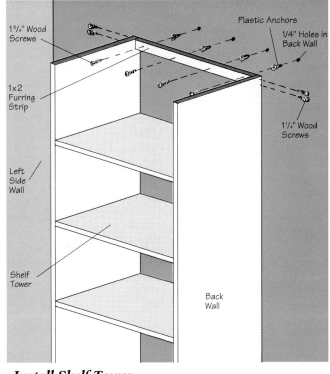

Install Shelf Tower

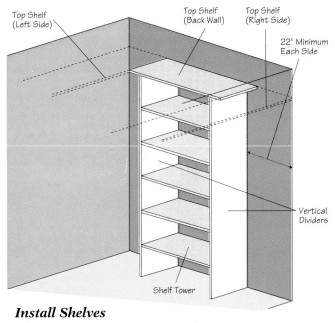

Install Shelves

only. Slide the other end into the slot cut in the opposite support (see page 102 for details). Repeat for the second upper rod, then for the lower rod. Finally, repeat the entire process for the right side wall (see illustration previous page for placement).

7 Install Shelves

Turn to page 102 for instructions on installing shelves above the rods. See page 42 for placement.

8 *Install Shoe Shelves*

Turn to page 107 for details on building and installing wooden, hand-built shoe shelves.

9 *Attach Trim Strips to Plywood*

Turn to page 103 for details on adding trim to the shelves.

Laminate Organizer

Time Required:	Novice 18 Hrs.	Average 12 Hrs.	Experienced 8 Hrs.

Tools & Materials (May vary according to manufacturer.)

☐ Variable Speed Drill with Screwdriver Bit or Screwdriver
☐ Hammer   ☐ Measuring Tape
☐ Pencil   ☐ Level
☐ (1 or 2) Shelf Towers (Optional)   ☐ (2) Shoe Shelves
☐ Stackable Shelves (Optional)   ☐ Individual Shelves
☐ Drawers
☐ (3) Shelves (Additional shelves optional)
☐ (5) Adjustable Rods (Additional rods optional)
Additional Items Needed (If not included in shelf tower kit):
☐ (2) Angle Brackets   ☐ (4) Plastic Anchors
☐ (4) 1" Wood Screws   ☐ (4) 3/4" Wood Screws

NOTE: *Instructions concerning the installation of laminated systems are manufacturer specific. Only general instructions are given here.*

1 *Install the Shelf Tower*

Shelf towers are available with or without drawers. First decide upon what kind you need. For details on laminated shelf towers, turn to page 108. You may prefer to install stackable or wire-coated shelves.

Measure the back wall and subtract the width of the shelf tower. (For wide closets, you may need to use two shelf towers. Subtract the combined width.) Divide the difference by two. The result must be at least 22", or the shelf tower is too wide. Measure the result from either side wall and place a mark on the back wall. Use a level to draw a vertical line at the mark. Assemble the shelf tower per the manufacturer's instructions and set in place with the left side on the line drawn on the back wall. Secure the tower to the back wall following the manufacturer's instructions, if provided. If not, secure with two angle brackets as detailed on page 108.

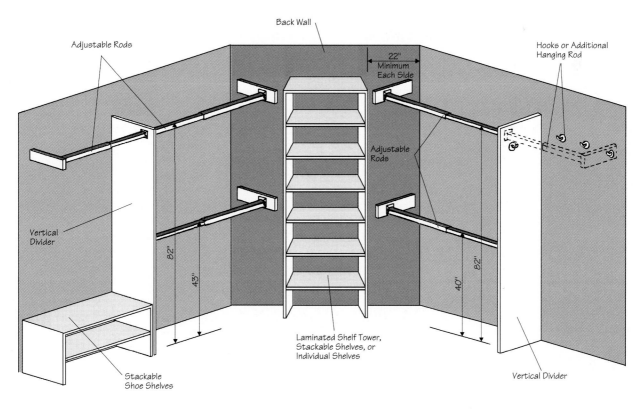

Laminate System

2 Install Rods

If using adjustable rods as shown in the drawing on the previous page, a vertical divider should be installed on both the left and right side walls, at 36" from the front wall (adjust for smaller closets). Install the laminate divider as directed by the manufacturer, or in the same manner as given for the shelf towers, see page 108. (Dividers also can be made of plywood if preferred.) With the vertical dividers in place, install two rods on the left wall at 82" above the floor. Use a level when installing the rods. The distance from the closet wall to the rod is 12".

Install a third rod at 43" above the floor, from the vertical divider to the back wall. On the right side, install one rod at the 82" and another at 40" above the floor, both from the vertical divider to the back wall. If not installing hooks, install an optional rod from the vertical divider to the front wall at 82" above the floor. For double hanging, install another rod at a lower height. For more on rods, see page 108.

3 Install Shelves

A shelf above the upper rods on both sides will provide additional storage space. Since this shelf is up high, it is perfect for storing out-of-season clothing or rarely used items. Determine the exact shelf arrangement, measure the length of the shelves, and then cut and install per the manufacturer's directions (see illustration page 42 for placement).

4 Install Hooks

The installation of hooks is optional. This design provides a place for hooks on the right side of the right wall. A guide to hooks is found on page 112.

5 Install Shoe Shelves

For details on installing shoe shelves, turn to page 108. See page 42 for placement.

Coated-Wire Organizer

Time Required:	Novice 18 Hrs.	Average 12 Hrs.	Experienced 8 Hrs.

Tools & Materials

☐ Variable Speed Drill with Screwdriver Bit or Screwdriver
☐ Hammer
☐ Measuring Tape
☐ Bolt Cutters or Hacksaw
☐ 16" Rod and Shelf (As needed)
☐ (20) Large End Caps
☐ (2) Sets Shoe Shelf Supports
☐ Down Clips
☐ Plastic Anchors
☐ 12" Support Braces (As needed)
☐ 12" Organizer Shelf for Shoe Shelves (As needed)
☐ 12" or 16" Organizer Shelf at Back Wall
☐ Joiner Plate Assemblies (As needed)
☐ 16" Support Braces (As needed)

☐ Pencil
☐ Level
☐ 12" Rod and Shelf (As needed)
☐ (76) Small End Caps
☐ (6) End Brackets
☐ Back Clips
☐ Screws
☐ Hooks

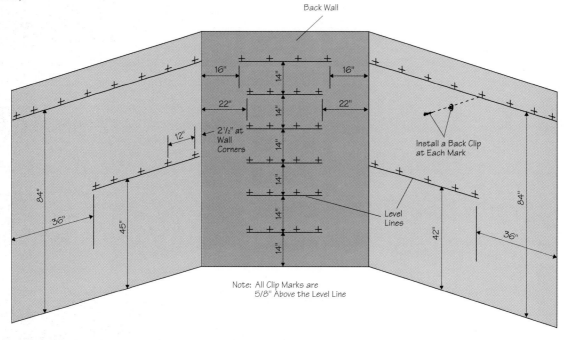

Back Wall

16"   14"   16"

22"   14"   22"

2½" at Wall Corners   14"

12"   14"

Install a Back Clip at Each Mark

84"   14"

36"   45"   14"

Level Lines

84"

14"   42"   36"

14"

Note: All Clip Marks are 5/8" Above the Level Line

Install Back Clips

1 Install Back Clips

Turn to pages 109-110 for a detailed look at a variety of clips and their installation. Measure 45" and 84" (adjust to the height of the user) up from the floor at the back left corner of the closet and place marks on the left wall. At the 45" mark use a level to draw a horizontal line along the left wall to 36" from the left side of the wall. (Adjust the 36" dimension for smaller closets.) Use the level again at the higher mark, drawing a horizontal line all the way across the left, right and back walls (see illustration previous page).

Measure 42" up from the floor at the back of the closet in the right corner and place a mark on the right wall. Use a level to draw a horizontal line along the right wall to 36" from the right side of the wall. On the back wall measure in 14" increments from the floor until reaching the 70" mark. (You can adjust these dimensions as desired, but do not put the shelves too close together or there will be an interference fit with the support braces. Test before installing permanently.) Draw a level, horizontal line through each mark. Stop the line 22" short of either side wall.

Starting with any line, make a mark at 5/8" above the line and 2½" from a side wall or 1" from an open end. Continue making marks 5/8" above the line and 12" apart until you reach the opposite end of the shelf line (2½" from a side wall). Complete this process for every line. Install a back clip at each mark for hollow or masonry walls. Use down clips for wood walls that are 1" thick or thicker.

2 Install Rods & Shelves (Side Walls)

Measure the length of the upper shelf on the left wall. Use bolt cutters to cut a piece of 16"-wide integral rod and shelf to the measured length less 1½". Slide end caps over the cut ends of the steel wires. The two steel wires that make up the clothes hanging part of the shelf require large end caps. The other three wires use small end caps.

Starting at either side wall and working one clip at a time, snap the shelf into the back clips. Repeat the process at the upper line on the right wall (for details, see pages 109-110). If any shelf is longer than 3½', install an additional support brace every 3½' starting from the back wall.

At the lower line on the left wall, measure the length of the shelf and cut 12" integral rod and shelf to the measured length less 3/4". Slide end caps onto the cut ends of the wires. Again, the two steel wires that make up the clothes hanging part of the shelf require large end caps. Snap into place as before. Install an end bracket at the right side wall and a 12" support brace at the left end of the shelf. Repeat the process for the lower line on the right wall.

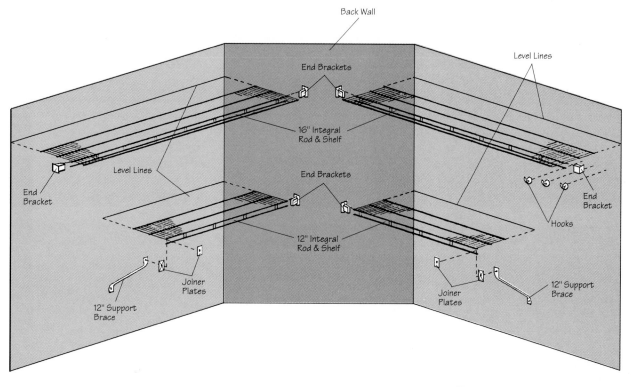

Install Rods & Shelves (Side Walls)

3 Install Rods & Shelves (Back Wall)

On the back wall, measure the distance between the 16" shelves on each side and cut a length of 16" integral rod and shelf or 16" organizer shelf to the measured distance less 1". (If you are going to hang clothes on the back wall, use integral rod and shelf. If you are going to install shelves as shown, either type of shelf may be used. Since the upper shelf will be tied to the upper shelves on the sides, you may want to use integral rod and shelf to match just for appearance sake.) Snap the shelf into the back clips on the upper level line. Install a support brace in the center of the shelf. Insert a corner bracket at each end of the shelf to tie it to the side shelves. Turn to page 111 for details on installing a corner support bracket.

For the remaining lines, cut the appropriate number of pieces of 16" organizer shelving (or 12" if preferred) to the length of the lines. Starting with the upper shelf, snap the shelf into the back clips and install a support brace at each end. It is doubtful that the shelves will be longer than 42", but if so install an additional brace every 3½'. Install all five 16" organizer shelves in this way. See illustration page 46 for placement.

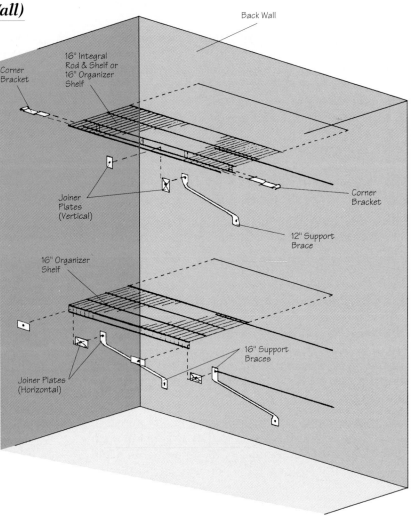

Install Rods & Shelves (Back Wall)

4 Install Additional Storage

The installation of hooks is optional. In this design the area for hooks is on the right side of the right wall, directly opposite the full-length hanging area. Install the hooks as detailed on page 112.

This area also can be used for hanging clothes if preferred, particularly since the upper integral rod and shelf is already in place. Simply extend the lower 12" integral rod and shelf for a double-hanging space.

5 Install Shoe Shelves

Two 36"-long shoe shelves will hold eight pairs of average-size shoes. Cut two pieces of 12" organizer shelf to 36" long each. For installation, follow the instructions found on page 111 (see illustration page 42 for placement).

Her Walk-In Closet

Women who own a large amount of clothing will find that a walk-in closet is an ideal solution. Even a small walk-in can provide plenty of changing space as well as ample drawer and shelf space. This design is based on a 6-foot-wide,

7-foot-deep walk-in closet, but will work equally as well for larger closets. For smaller walk-ins reduce the width of the shelves. For much larger walk-ins consider developing a more elaborate design.

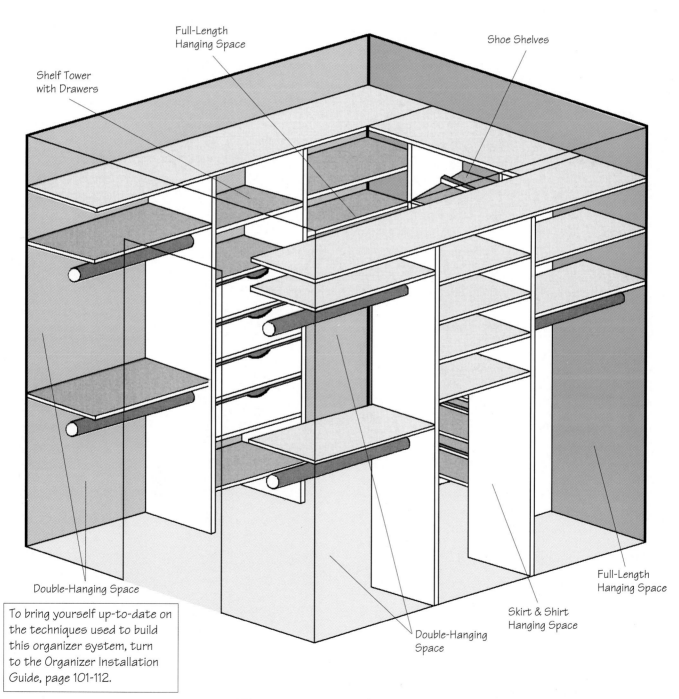

Shelf Tower with Drawers

Full-Length Hanging Space

Shoe Shelves

Double-Hanging Space

Double-Hanging Space

Skirt & Shirt Hanging Space

Full-Length Hanging Space

To bring yourself up-to-date on the techniques used to build this organizer system, turn to the Organizer Installation Guide, page 101-112.

Hand-Built Organizer

Time Required:	Novice	Average	Experienced
	20 Hrs.	14 Hrs.	9 Hrs.

Tools & Materials

☐ Variable Speed Drill with Screwdriver Bit or Screwdriver
☐ Hammer
☐ Measuring Tape
☐ Combination Square
☐ Framing Square
☐ Pencil
☐ Utility Knife
☐ Table Saw (Optional)
☐ Circular Saw
☐ Level
☐ Miter Saw
☐ Crosscut (Hand) Saw
☐ Hanging Rod (As needed)
☐ 3/4" Screen Mold
☐ Paint or Stain
☐ 1¼" Wood Screws
☐ 1¾" Wood Screws
☐ 4d Finishing Nails
☐ 2d Finishing Nails
☐ Carpenter's Glue
☐ Sandpaper
☐ (4 or 5) Sheets 3/4" Plywood (Cut into 3 strips, 16" wide)
☐ 1x2 Furring - 1x1 or 45-degree Trim Also May Be Used (As needed)
☐ 1x4 - Clear Grade or Number 1 Grade (As needed)
☐ 1x1 or Smaller Stock (For heel stop)

NOTE: *If the organizer is not going to be painted the same color as the closet, it is suggested that you first sand, then paint or stain the material before installing, and touch up afterward. This will be much easier than trying to paint precise lines where the organizer meets the closet walls.*

1 Select & Cut Plywood

The first step in building the organizer is to obtain the wood for the project. A guide to selecting and cutting plywood is found on page 101.

2 Install Side Wall Shelf Towers

The design shown features a 24" shelf tower on each side wall. You may need to vary the width of the shelf tower because of a different closet depth or to suit individual needs. The tower for the left side wall contains a combination of shelves and drawers. Cut two strips of plywood to 83¼" long for the left side wall shelf tower. Determine the shelf and drawer arrangement that suits you best, then multiply the number of shelves by two and cut as many 12" long 1x2 furring strips. (You can also use 1x1 or 45-degree trim for the furring strips.)   Install the furring strips in the shelf tower at the desired locations with 1¼" wood screws (see 102-104 for more details on building a shelf tower).

Measure 30" from the front wall on the left side wall and use a level to draw a plumb, vertical line through the mark. Install the tower at the vertical line as detailed on page 105.

Use a level to draw horizontal lines from the top of the shelf tower all along the back wall and both side walls. Extend the lines 16" onto the front wall at each side. Measure 30" from the front wall on the right side wall and draw another plumb, vertical line. The tower for the right side wall does not have any divisions at this time. This is because it is designed to contain a hanging rod at the bottom and it will be easier to install the rod after the tower is installed (the shelves will be put in place after the rod is installed). Measure the distance from the floor to the horizontal line at the top. Construct a shelf tower to this height and install as before. You may install furring strips for the shelves, but do not install the shelves at this time.

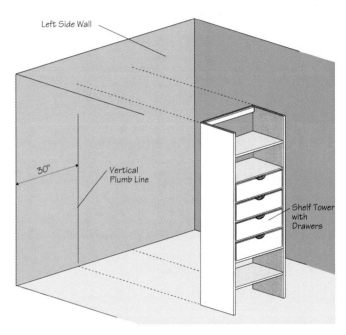

Install Shelf Tower (Left)

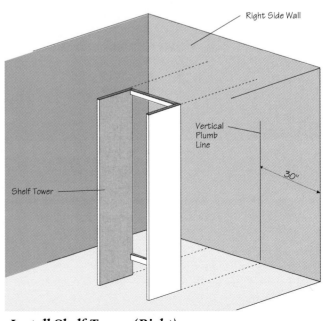

Install Shelf Tower (Right)

3 Install Rod & Shelf Supports (Left)

Measure up 59¼" from the floor at the right side of the left side wall and place a mark. Place another mark 12" higher. On the left side of the left wall, measure 35¼" and 71¼" and place marks. Use a level to draw lines along the side wall at the marks. Continue the lines 16" onto the front and back walls and along the shelf tower sides. Be sure all lines are level.

Construct three pairs of rod and shelf supports as detailed on page 101. For a walk-in closet, all rod and shelf supports should be 16" long. Install two pairs on the left side of the shelf tower at the two lower level lines. On the right side, install a single pair of rod and shelf supports at the lower line.

4 Install Rod & Shelf Supports (Right)

Measure 41¼" and 77¼" up from the floor on the right side of the right side wall and draw level lines. Draw a line at 59¼" on the left side of the right wall. Draw an additional line 12" higher. In the shelf tower, draw a line at 47¼" above the floor, then at 9" increments above the lower line. Construct four more pairs of rod and shelf supports. Install as shown.

5 Install Rods

Measure the distance from side to side at any rod location. Cut a length of rod to fit and insert one end into the support with the drilled hole only. Slide the other end into the slot cut in the opposite support. Repeat for all remaining pairs of rod and shelf supports.

6 Install Shelves

For details on installing shelves see page 102, then return to finish the step.

Install long shelves on top of the shelf tower on each side wall. These shelves should extend from the front wall to the back wall (see illustration page 49 for placement).

7 Install Shoe Shelves

Measure the width of the back wall and subtract 44". The remaining distance is the maximum width of the shelf tower. You may prefer to narrow the shelf tower further to allow easier access to the hanging space on each side. Measure the distance from the floor to the top level line. Cut two strips of plywood to that length. Install a furring strip at the top and

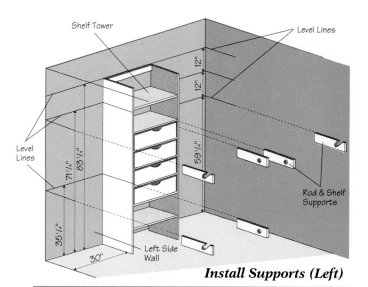

Install Supports (Left)

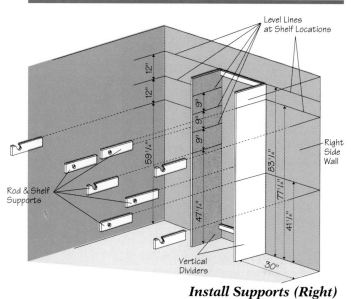

Install Supports (Right)

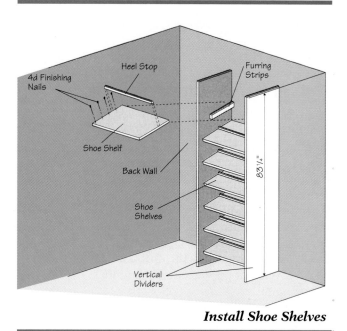

Install Shoe Shelves

bottom and install the tower on the back wall in the same manner as before.

Cut and install a shoe shelf furring strip (see page 107) every 11" on both vertical dividers, using a level to ensure that the strips are level with each other. Measure the inside width and cut shelving to fit. Install a heel stop on the shelves with 2d finishing nails, then install the shelves starting at the bottom. Use four 4d finishing nails each end of each shelf. Finally, install a shelf on top of the tower between the top shelves on the side walls. Nail the shelf into the vertical dividers of the tower with 4d finishing nails. Toenail the shelf into the side shelves to tie the top shelf together.

8 *Attach Trim Strips to Plywood*

Turn to the page 103 for details on adding trim to hand-built shelves.

Laminate Organizer

Time Required:	Novice	Average	Experienced
	10 Hrs.	7 Hrs.	4 Hrs.

Tools & Materials

☐ Variable Speed Drill with Screwdriver Bit or Screwdriver
☐ Hammer ☐ Measuring Tape
☐ Pencil ☐ Level
☐ (2) Shelf Towers
☐ (7) Adjustable Rods (Additional rods optional)
☐ Stackable Shoe Shelves
☐ (8) Shelves (Additional shelves optional)
Additional Items Needed (If not included in shelf tower kit):
☐ (2) Angle Brackets ☐ (4) Plastic Anchors
☐ (4) 1" Wood Screws ☐ (4) 3/4" Wood Screws

NOTE: *Instructions for the installation of laminated systems are manufacturer specific. Only general instructions are given here.*

1 *Install Shelf Towers*

There is a 24"-wide shelf tower on each wall of this closet. For information on laminated shelf towers, turn to page 108. Adjust as necessary to accommodate the depth of your closet and to meet individual needs. Build the shelf towers according to manufacturer's instructions. Install shelves, drawers and hooks. Secure the shelf towers to the center of the left and right side walls. If the manufacturer has not provided a method for securing the shelf tower, follow the directions on page 108.

2 *Install Rods & Shelves (Left)*

Install one rod on the right side of the shelf tower on the left side wall at 58" above the floor. On the left side of the shelf tower, install rods at 34" and 70" above the floor. Use a level when installing the rods. The distance from the left side wall to the rod is 12". It is parallel to the rod.

A shelf above the upper rods on both sides of the shelf tower and an additional shelf 12" above the shelf on the right side will provide extra space for folding clothes, hats and other items. Also, install a long shelf all the way across the closet on top of the shelf tower (84" above the floor). This upper level may be better used for items that are not worn often.

Determine the exact shelf arrangement, measure the length of the shelves, then cut and install per the manufacturer's directions. For more information on adjustable rods, turn to page 108.

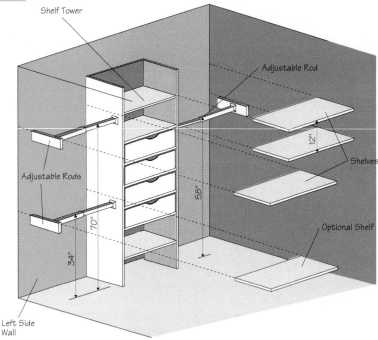

Install Shelf Tower, Rods & Shelves (Left)

3 *Install Stackable Shoe Shelves*

Measure the back wall and subtract 44". The difference is the maximum width of the stackable shoe shelves. Assemble and install the shoe shelves of your choice (see page 49 for placement). For more on laminated shoe shelves see page 108.

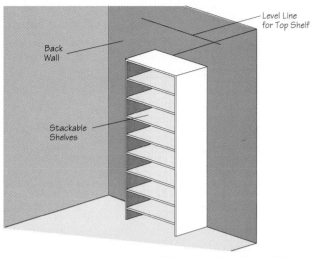

Install Stackable Shoe Shelves

4 *Install Rods & Shelves (Right)*

On the right side wall, install adjustable or fixed rods at 40" and 76" above the floor on the right side of the shelf tower and at 50" above the floor on the left side of the shelf tower. Install another rod at 48" above the floor in the shelf tower. Install shelves in the same manner as was done on the left side wall.

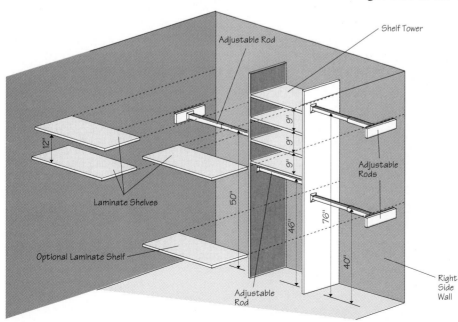

Install Rods & Shelves (Right)

Coated-Wire Organizer

Time Required:	Novice	Average	Experienced
	8 Hrs.	5 Hrs.	3 Hrs.

Tools & Materials

☐ Variable Speed Drill with Screwdriver Bit or Screwdriver
☐ Hammer   ☐ Pencil
☐ Measuring Tape   ☐ Level
☐ Bolt Cutters or Hacksaw   ☐ 12" Rod and Shelf (As needed)
☐ (148) Small End Caps   ☐ (28) Large End Caps
☐ (11) End Brackets   ☐ (2) Corner Brackets
☐ (6) Sets Shoe Shelf Support ☐ (2) Cross Brace Sets
☐ Wire-Basket Drawers   ☐ Drawer Stops (As needed)
☐ (1) Set Casters (Optional) ☐ Down Clips
☐ Screws   ☐ Plastic Anchors
☐ Hooks   ☐ Back Clips
☐ 12" Support Braces (As needed)
☐ 12" Organizer Shelf for Shoe Shelves (As needed)
☐ 12" or 16" Organizer Shelf at Back Wall
☐ 16" Support Braces (As needed)
☐ Joiner Plate Assemblies (As needed)
☐ (2) 7-Runner Side Frame Sets
☐ (1) Set Floor Protectors (If not using casters)
☐ (1) Set Leg Extensions-For Casters (Optional)
☐ (1) Drawer System Top (Optional)

1 *Install Back Clips*

Left Side Wall: Measure 60", 72" and 84" (adjust to the height of the user) up from the floor at the right side of the left wall and place marks on the left wall. At the 60" mark use a level to draw a 30"-long horizontal line along the left wall starting on the right side of the wall. (Adjust the horizontal measurements for different size closets or to suit individual needs.) Draw another 30" line at the 72" mark. Use the level again at the higher mark, drawing a horizontal line all the way across the left, back and right walls. Measure 36" and 72" up from the floor at the left side of the left wall and place marks on the wall. Draw 30"-long lines at the marks, starting from the left side of the wall. The width of the area between the lower lines should be about 24".

Back Wall: Starting at the floor near the center of the wall, measure in 12" increments up to 72".

Use a level at each mark to draw a line to a minimum of 22" from each side wall.

Right Side Wall: On the left side of the right side wall measure 60" and 72" up from the floor. Starting at the left side of the wall draw 30"-long level lines at both marks. On the right side of the wall measure up 42" and 78" from the floor. Draw 30"-long lines through the marks. In the center of the wall, measure up 48", then in increments of 9", draw level lines through the marks between the previous lines. Install the clips using the guide on pages 109-110.

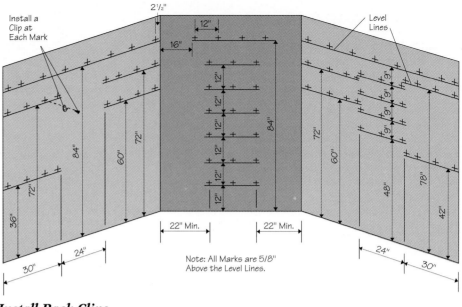

Install Back Clips

2 *Install Side Wall Shelves (Left)*

Measure the length of the upper shelf on the left wall. Use bolt cutters to cut a piece of 16"-wide organizer shelf to the measured length less 1½". Slide small end caps over the cut ends of the steel wires.

Starting at either side wall and working one clip at a time, snap the shelf into place in the back clips. Install an end bracket at each end of the shelf and support braces every 3½' along the shelf. See page 110 for installation details.

At the 72" line on the right side of the left side wall, install 16" organizer shelf. At the remaining three lines install 12" integral rod and shelf. Each of the

four shelves should be cut to 3/4" less than the measured length. Slide end caps onto the cut ends of the wires. The two steel wires that make up the clothes hanging part of the integral rod and shelf require large end caps. Use small end caps on the remaining cut wires. Snap the shelves into place as before. Install end brackets where the shelves meet the wall and support braces at the open ends. If any shelf is longer than 3½', install an additional support brace every 3½'.

3 *Install Drawer System*

Assemble the wire-basket drawer system as detailed on page 112. Set in place at the end of the lower rod.

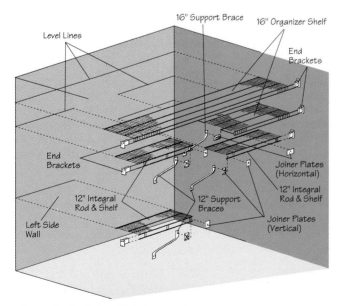

Install Shelves (Left)

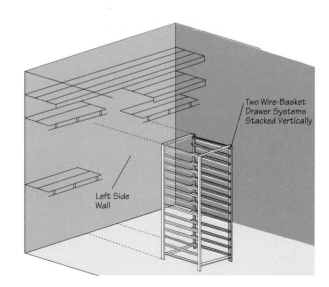

Install Drawer System (Left)

4 Install Side Wall Shelves (Right)

Install a 16" organizer shelf at the top line on the right side in the same manner as before. Install a 12" integral rod and shelf at the two lines on the right side and the lower line on the left side of the wall. Cut the shelves to 3/4" less than the measured length for shelves that abut a wall on one end. Install a 12" organizer shelf at the remaining line on the left side of the right side wall.

Note: *Do not install support braces at the open ends of the shelves. The open ends on the right side wall will be held in place by support poles.*

In the center, install a 12" integral rod and shelf at the lower line and 12" organizer shelving at the remaining lines. Install two support poles as explained on page 111 to support the open ends of the shelves. If any shelf is longer than 42" install support braces every 3½' along the shelf except where supported by a pole.

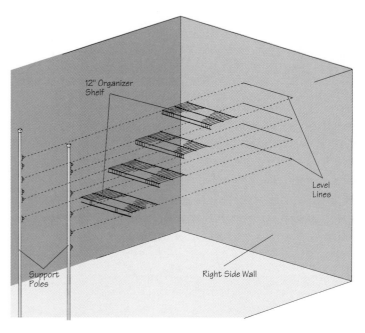

Install Shelves (Right Center)

5 Install Back Wall Shelves

Measure the length of the shoe shelf lines at the back wall. Remember the lines should be no closer than 22" to either side wall. Cut six pieces of 12" organizer shelf to the measured lengths. Install a pair of shoe shelf supports on the shelf, then snap the shelf into the clips at the lower line. Lower it into position with the supports resting against the wall surface (see page 111 for details). Install the remaining shelves in the same manner as the first.

Measure the distance between the top shelf on each side wall. Cut 16" organizer shelving to 1" less than the measured distance. Install into the back clips at the top line. Lower and install a corner support bracket at each end of the shelf as explained on page 111. Install a 16" support brace in the middle of the shelf or if the shelf is longer than 7', install support braces every 3½' along the shelf.

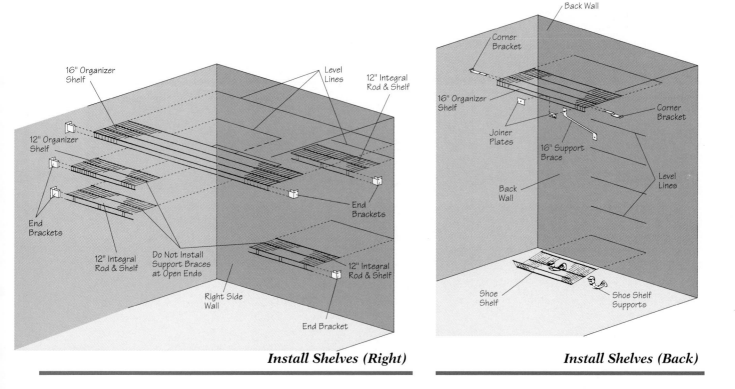

Install Shelves (Right) *Install Shelves (Back)*

His & Her Walk-In Closet

For a man and a woman who share a closet, a walk-in is a luxury. This type of closet can be accessed by both people at the same time. Approximately one third of it is designed for the man's needs and two thirds is designed for the woman's needs. This project is based on a typical 6-foot-wide, 7-foot-deep walk-in, but will work equally as well for larger closets. For smaller walk-ins reduce the 36" dimension for the full-length and hook-hanging areas. For much larger walk-ins consider developing a more elaborate design.

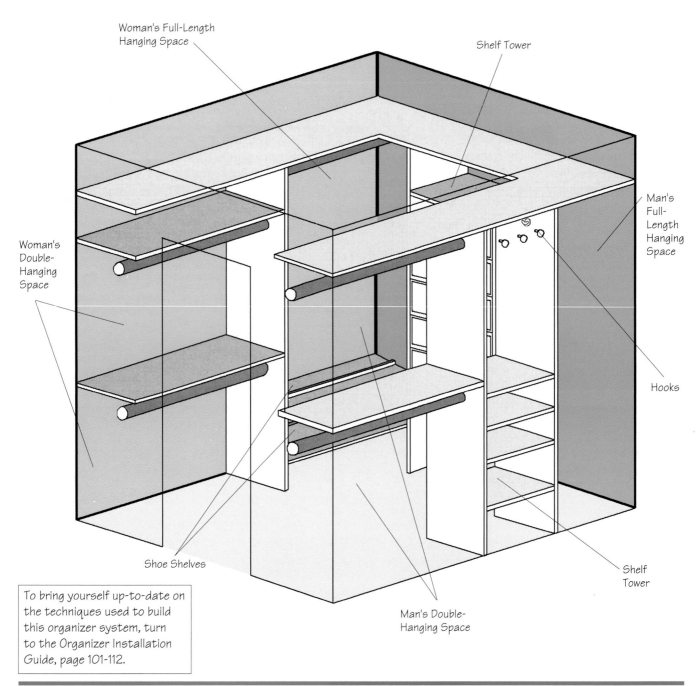

Woman's Full-Length Hanging Space

Shelf Tower

Woman's Double-Hanging Space

Man's Full-Length Hanging Space

Hooks

Shoe Shelves

Shelf Tower

Man's Double-Hanging Space

To bring yourself up-to-date on the techniques used to build this organizer system, turn to the Organizer Installation Guide, page 101-112.

Hand-Built Organizer

Time Required:	Novice	Average	Experienced
	18 Hrs.	12 Hrs.	8 Hrs.

Tools & Materials

☐ Variable Speed Drill with Screwdriver Bit or Screwdriver
☐ Hammer
☐ Combination Square
☐ Pencil
☐ Table Saw (Optional)
☐ Level Miter Saw
☐ Hanging Rod (As needed)
☐ Paint or Stain
☐ 1³/₄" Wood Screws
☐ 2d Finishing Nails
☐ Sandpaper
☐ Measuring Tape
☐ Framing Square
☐ Utility Knife
☐ Circular Saw
☐ Crosscut (Hand) Saw
☐ 3/4" Screen Molding
☐ 1¹/₄" Wood Screws
☐ 4d Finishing Nails
☐ Carpenter's Glue
☐ (4) Sheets 3/4" Plywood (Cut into 3 strips, 16" wide)
☐ 1x2 Furring - 1x1 or 45-degree Trim Also May Be Used (As needed)
☐ 1x4 - Clear Grade or Number 1 Grade (As needed)
☐ 1x1 or Smaller Stock for Heel Stop (Optional)
Additional Items Needed to Secure Each Vertical Divider to the Wall:
☐ (2) Angle Brackets
☐ (4) 1" Wood Screws
☐ (4) Plastic Anchors
☐ (4) 3/4" Wood Screws

NOTE: *If the organizer is not going to be painted the same color as the closet, it is suggested that you sand first, then paint or stain before installing, and touch up afterward. This will be much easier than trying to paint precise lines where the organizer meets the closet walls.*

1 Select & Cut Plywood

The first step in building the organizer is to obtain the wood. A guide to selecting and cutting plywood is found on page 101.

2 Install Shelf Towers

The man's shelf tower is located on the right side wall. It is 18" wide and contains hooks in the upper section and shelves in the lower section. The woman's shelf tower is placed at the back wall. It is 24" wide and contains a combination of drawers and shelves. Adjust the tower widths and construction to meet your particular needs.

Cut two strips of plywood to 83¹/₄" long. Determine the shelf arrangement you want in the man's shelf tower, then multiply the number of shelves by two and cut as many 12"-long 1x2 furring strips. (You also can use 1x1 or 45-degree trim for the furring strips.) Construct the shelf tower as detailed on pages 102-104. For an 18"-wide shelf tower, use shelves that are 16¹/₂" long. Install the bottom shelf first and work up one shelf at a time.

Measure 24" from the left side of the right wall and use a level to draw a plumb vertical line at the mark.

Set the tower in place with the left side of the tower on the vertical line. As detailed on page 105, add two furring strips to the back of the tower, at the top and bottom, and secure to the wall with plastic anchors and 1³/₄" wood screws.

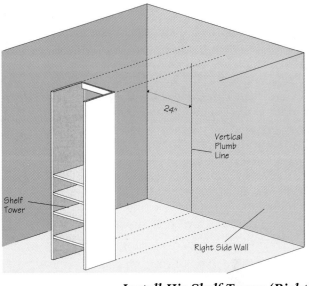

Install His Shelf Tower (Right)

Use a level to draw a horizontal line from the top of the shelf tower all the way around both side walls and the back wall. At the back wall measure the distance from the floor to the line. Cut two strips of 16"-wide plywood to the measured distance. These are the vertical dividers for the woman's shelf tower. Build the tower to 24" wide as shown on pages 102-104. Drawers can be constructed as detailed on pages 105-106. Measure the back wall of the closet and subtract the width of the shelf tower. Divide the

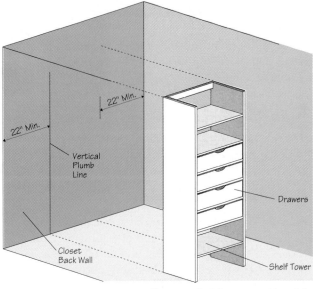

Install Her Shelf Tower (Back)

difference by two. Measure the result (minimum of 22") over from either side wall and use a level to draw a plumb vertical line. Set the tower in place and secure it in the same manner as before.

3 Install Supports (Left)

At the center of the left side wall measure the distance from the floor to the level line. Cut a strip of 16"-wide plywood to the measured length. This is the vertical divider. Install the divider in the same manner as explained for a laminated shelf tower on page 108. Measure up 35¼" and 71¼" from the floor at the left side of the left wall and place marks on the wall. Use a level to draw horizontal lines from the front wall to the vertical divider at each line. Continue the level lines 16" along the front wall and along the vertical divider.

Construct three pairs of rod and shelf supports as detailed on page 101. All rod and shelf supports should be 16" long. Install two pairs on the left side of the closet at the two lower level lines, as shown. On the right side install the remaining pair of rod and shelf supports at the top line. Finally, cut a pair of 16"-long furring strips and install at the top line on the left side of the vertical divider.

4 Install Supports (Right)

Measure up 44¼" from the floor on the right side of the shelf tower and draw a level line in the same manner as before. Build three pairs of rod and shelf supports. Install two pairs on the right side of the shelf tower and one on the left at the level lines. Then, install the hooks in the shelf tower as detailed page 112.

5 Install Rods & Shelves

Turn to page 102 for details on building and installing the rods and shelves.

6 Install Shoe Shelves

Measure the distance from the vertical divider to the back wall on the left side wall at 8" and 18" above the floor. Cut two shelves to the measured length. Turn to page 107 for details on building and installing the shoe shelves (see illustration page 56 for placement).

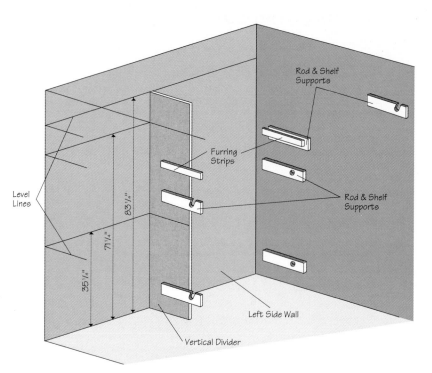

Install Supports (Left)

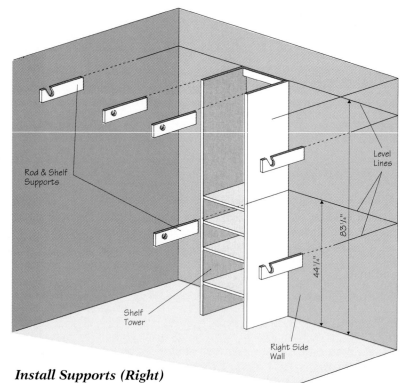

Install Supports (Right)

7 Attach Trim Strips to Plywood

Turn to page 103 for details on adding trim to the plywood.

Laminate Organizer

Time Required:	Novice	Average	Experienced
	9 Hrs.	6 Hrs.	3 Hrs.

Tools & Materials

☐ Variable Speed Drill with Screwdriver Bit or Screwdriver
☐ Hammer   ☐ Measuring Tape
☐ Pencil   ☐ Level
☐ (6) Adjustable Rods   ☐ Shoe Shelves
☐ (2) Shelf Towers
☐ (4) Shelves (Additional shelves optional)

Additional Items Needed (If not included in the shelf tower kit):

☐ (2) Angle Brackets   ☐ (4) Plastic Anchors
☐ (4) 1" Wood Screws   ☐ (4) 3/4" Wood Screws

NOTE: *Instructions for the installation of laminated systems are manufacturer specific. Only general instructions are given here.*

1 Install Rods & Shelves (Left)

Install a vertical divider on the left side wall at 42" from the front wall (adjust for smaller closets). Install the laminate divider as per manufacturer's instruction, or in the same manner as described for plywood on page 43.

With the vertical divider in place, install two rods on the left side of the left wall at 34" and 70" above the floor. Use a level when installing the rods. The distance from the left side wall to the rod is 12". Install a third rod at 82" above the floor, from the vertical divider to the back wall (see page 108 for more details).

A shelf at the top and another above the upper rod on the left side of the wall will provide additional space. The upper level may be better used for items that are not worn often. Determine the exact shelf arrangement, measure the length of the shelves, then cut and install per the manufacturer's directions.

If you choose to add shoe shelves, assemble and install per the manufacturer's directions. See page 108 for more details.

2 Install Shelf Tower

For more details on laminated shelf towers, turn to page 108.

Starting from the back wall, measure 24" along the right side wall. Using a level, draw a plumb vertical line at the mark. Assemble the shelf tower per the manufacturer's directions and set in place with the left side of the tower on the vertical line. Secure to the wall following the manufacturer's directions, if provided. If not, secure with two angle brackets as detailed on page 108.

3 Install Rods & Shelves (Right)

Install an adjustable rod at 43" and 82" above the floor on the right side of the shelf tower. Use a level to ensure that the rods are level. Install a third rod on the left side of the shelf tower at the 82" mark. Install a full-length shelf all the way across the right side wall on top of the shelf tower. An optional shelf can be installed above the lower rod on the left side, but the clothes may hang too low for this rod to be used for storage.

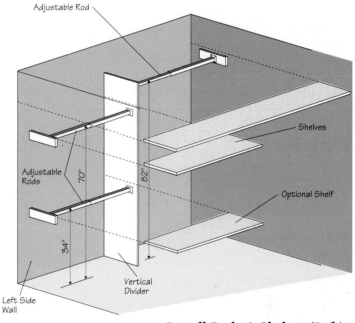

Install Rods & Shelves (Left)

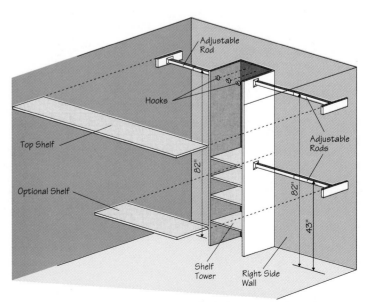

Install Rods & Shelves (Right)

4 *Install Hooks*

The installation of hooks is optional. This design provides a place for hooks in the shelf tower on the right wall. A guide to hooks is found on page 112.

5 *Install Back Wall Shelf Tower*

Measure the width of the back wall and subtract 44". The result is the maximum width of the back wall shelf tower. You may prefer to use a narrower tower to allow easier access to the hanging areas on either side. Subtract the width of the shelf tower you will use from the width of the back wall and divide the answer by two. Measure the result from either side wall and place a mark on the back wall. Use a level to draw a plumb vertical line at the mark. Assemble the shelf tower per the manufacturer's directions and set in place in the closet with the one side on the line drawn on the back wall. Secure to the back wall following the manufacturer's directions, if provided. If not, secure with two angle brackets as detailed on page 108 (see the hand-built shelf tower illustration at the bottom of page 57 for placement). You may prefer to install stackable shelves.

Coated-Wire Organizer

Time Required:	Novice	Average	Experienced
	6 Hrs.	4 Hrs.	2 Hrs.

Tools & Materials

☐ Variable Speed Drill with Screwdriver Bit or Screwdriver

☐ Hammer

☐ Measuring Tape

☐ (46) Small End Caps

☐ (6) End Brackets

☐ Back Clips

☐ Plastic Anchors

☐ (24) Large End Caps

☐ 12" Support Braces (As needed)

☐ (2) Sets Shoe Shelf Supports

☐ Bolt Cutters or Hacksaw

☐ 12" Rod and Shelf (As needed)

☐ 16" Rod and Shelf (As needed)

☐ 12" Organizer Shelf for Shoe Shelves (As needed)

☐ 16" Support Braces (As needed)

☐ Joiner Plate Assemblies (As needed)

☐ Pencil

☐ Level

☐ Hooks

☐ Screws

☐ Down Clips

1 *Install Back Clips*

Measure 36", 72" and 84" (adjust for the height of the user) up from the floor at the left edge of the left side wall and place marks on the wall. At the 36" and 72" marks use a level to draw 42"-long horizontal lines, starting from the left edge. (Adjust the 42" dimension for smaller closets.) Use the level again at the higher mark, drawing a horizontal line all the way across the left wall, the back wall and the right wall.

Measure 12" and 24" up from the floor at the right edge of the left side wall. Draw level lines from the right edge of the wall to a point even with the ends of the previously drawn lines. Measure 45" up from the floor at the right edge of the right side wall and draw a 42"-long line starting from the right edge.

Install the clips according to instructions on page 109.

2 *Install Wall Shelves (Left)*

Measure the length of the upper shelf on the left wall. Use bolt cutters to cut a piece of 16"-wide integral rod and shelf to the measured length less 1¹/₂". Slide end caps over the cut ends of the steel wires. The two steel wires that make up the clothes hanging part of the shelf require large end caps. The other three wires use small end caps.

Starting at either side wall and working one clip at a time, snap the shelf into place in the back clips as demonstrated on page 110.

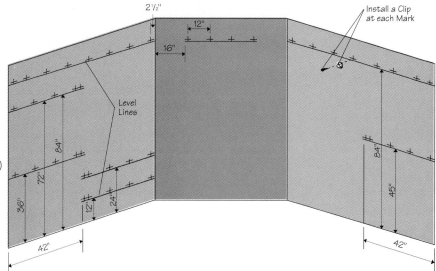

Install Back Clips

At the two lower lines on the left side of the left wall, measure the length of the shelves and cut 12" integral rod and shelf to the measured length less 3/4". Slide end caps onto the cut ends of the wires. Install an end bracket at the front wall and a 12" support brace at the right end of each shelf. If any shelf is longer than 3½', install an additional support brace every 3½', see page 110 for details.

Measure the length of the two lines at the lower right corner of the left wall. Cut two pieces of 12" organizer shelf to the measured length. These are the shoe shelves as detailed on page 111.

3 *Install Shelves & Drawers*

Measure the length of the upper level line and cut a piece of 16" integral rod and shelf to the measured length less 1½". Install the shelf as before, using an end bracket at each end and 12" support braces every 3½' along the shelf. Install a 12" integral rod and shelf at the lower line on the right side of the wall. Use an end bracket at the front wall and a 12" support brace at the open end of the shelf.

Assemble a 17"-wide, 10-runner wire-basket drawer system as explained on page 112. Slide into place at the end of the lower shelf.

4 *Install Hanging Hooks*

The installation of hooks is optional. In this design the area for hooks is in the center of the right side wall, above the drawer system. Install the hooks as detailed on page 112. If preferred, this area can be used for hanging clothes, particularly since the upper integral rod and shelf is already in place.

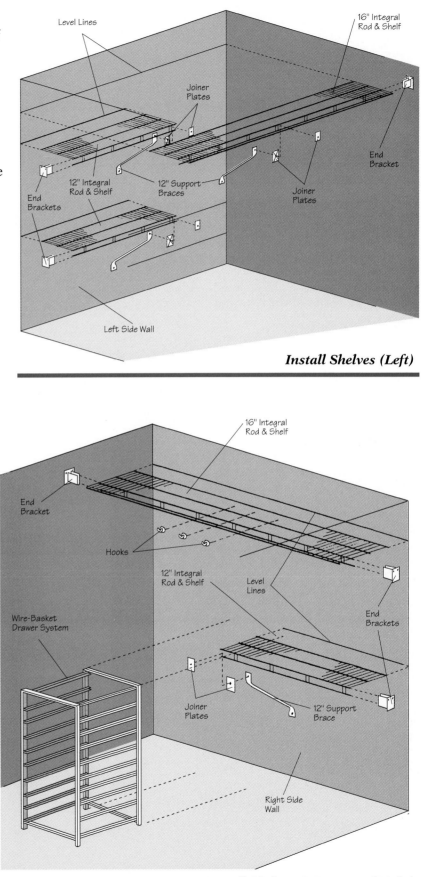

Install Shelves (Left)

Install Shelves & Drawers (Right)

5 *Install Shelf & Drawers*

On the back wall, measure the distance between the 16" shelves on each side and cut a length of 16" integral rod and shelf to the measured distance less 1". Snap the shelf into the back clips on the upper level line. Install a support brace in the center of the shelf. Insert a corner bracket at each end of the shelf to tie it to the side shelves. Turn to page 111 for details on how to install a corner support bracket.

Assemble two 22"-wide 7-runner wire-basket drawer systems as explained on page 112. Slide into place in the center of the rear wall.

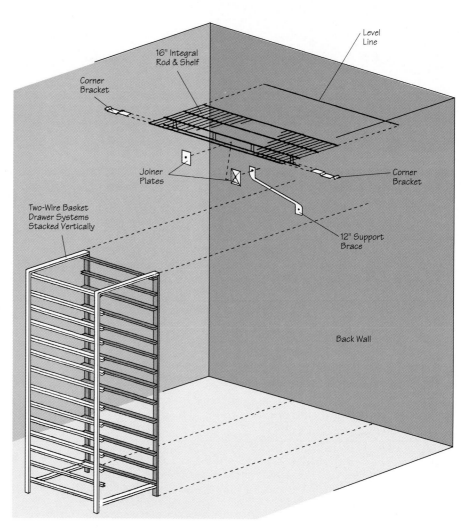

Level Line

16" Integral Rod & Shelf

Corner Bracket

Joiner Plates

Corner Bracket

12" Support Brace

Two-Wire Basket Drawer Systems Stacked Vertically

Back Wall

Install Shelf & Drawers (Back)

Carousel-Style Closet

For homes that are short on storage space, the answer may be a carousel or revolving closet. This type of organizer uses virtually all of the closet volume for storage and is operated by a switch outside of the closet.

Although they are expensive, revolving organizers make optimum use of small and large spaces, and could prove well worth the higher cost, in comparison to the cost of constructing additional space.

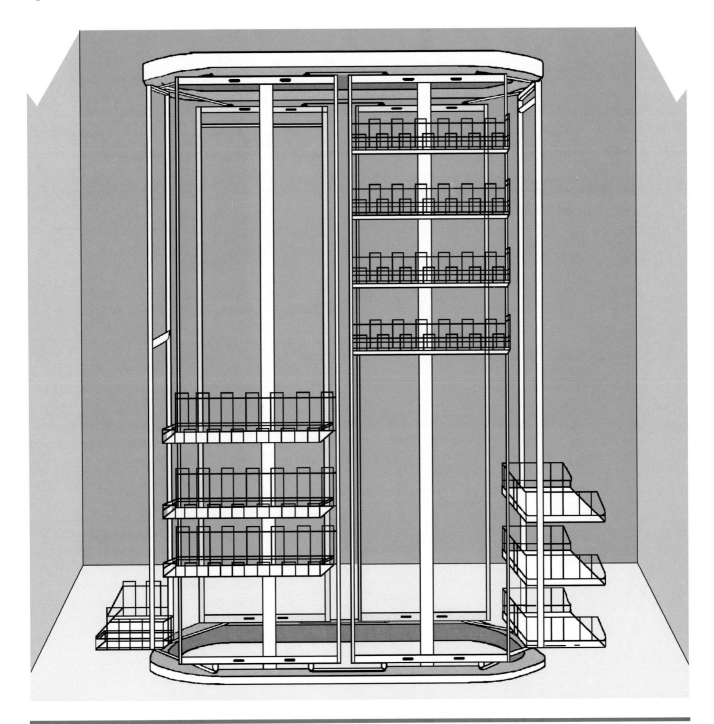

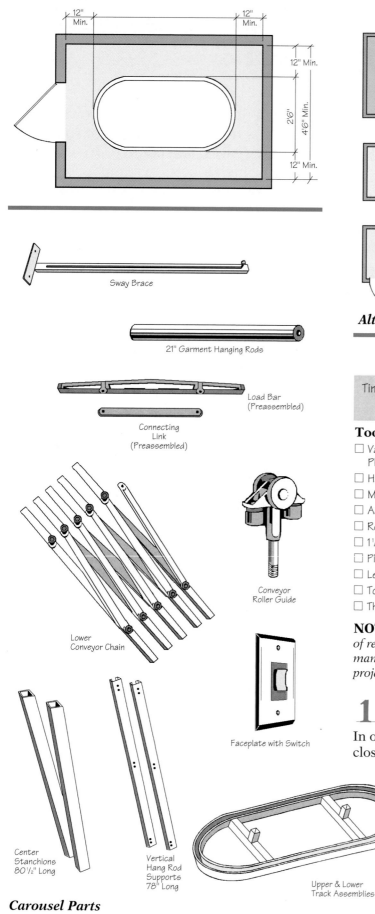

Sway Brace

21" Garment Hanging Rods

Load Bar
(Preassembled)

Connecting
Link
(Preassembled)

Conveyor
Roller Guide

Lower
Conveyor Chain

Faceplate with Switch

Center
Stanchions
80½" Long

Vertical
Hang Rod
Supports
78" Long

Upper & Lower
Track Assemblies

Carousel Parts

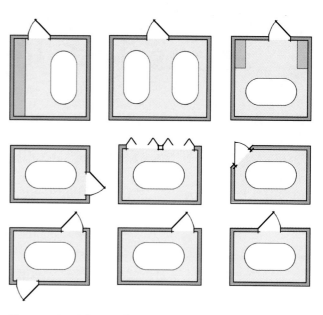

Alternative Floor Plans

Time Required:	Novice	Average	Experienced
	12 Hrs.	8 Hrs.	4 Hrs.

Tools & Materials

☐ Variable Speed Drill with Screwdriver Bits or
  Phillips and Flat Blade Screwdrivers
☐ Hammer   ☐ Pencil
☐ Measuring Tape   ☐ Level
☐ Adjustable Open-End Wrench ☐ Pliers
☐ Revolving Closet Kit
☐ 1¼" Wood Screws (For securing lower track to floor)
☐ Plastic Anchors (Masonry floors only)
☐ Leveling Shims (If floor is not level)
☐ Toggle Bolts or Wall Anchors (For securing sway braces to wall)
☐ Three Conductor 18-Gauge Wire (As needed)

NOTE: *The following are guidelines for installing one type of revolving organizer system. Carefully read through the manufacturer's instructions before installing the unit. This project requires two workers.*

1 Prepare for Installation

In order to install a revolving closet organizer, the closet must be a minimum of 4'6" wide. The amount of depth necessary will vary depending on the unit purchased. The shortest system, and the one most commonly used in homes, requires a minimum depth of 6'. The minimum ceiling height is 7'5", though some companies offer custom designs (see chart next page). The illustrations above show a variety of installation plans.

Carefully check the closet walls for nails, screws, trim or other protruding items. The walls must be smooth and clean to avoid any damage to clothing.

Closet Dimensions

Min. Width	Min. Length	No. of Hanging Sections	No. of Center Stanchions
4'6"	6'	5	2
"	7'	6	2
"	8'	7	2
"	9'	8	2
"	10'	9	3
"	11'	10	3
"	12'	11	3
"	13'	12	4
"	14'	13	4
"	15'	14	4
"	16'	15	5
"	17'	16	5

2 Install Lower Track Assembly

Set the lower track assembly on the floor and center between the side walls, then the front and back walls. There should be a minimum clearance of 12" on all four walls. The lower track can be installed directly over the finish flooring, including carpet. Check the unit with a level. If it is not level, you can use shims to level the unit, but be careful not to warp the track as this would impede operation.

Once level, secure to the floor. For wood floors install with 1¹/₄" wood screws through the predrilled holes in the track. For masonry floors, mark the hole locations then remove the track. Drill 1/4" holes with a masonry bit and install plastic anchors. Set the track back into place and secure to the plastic anchors with 1¹/₄" wood screws. It is very important that the installed track is level. Finally, place the center stanchions in the stanchion brackets on the lower track assembly.

3 Install Upper Track Assembly

First, decide where you want the drive assembly located. It should be in a location that is not easily visible from the closet door. Locate the drive assembly mounting holes in the upper track assembly, then orient the assembly accordingly.

Lifting the upper track assembly requires at least two people, depending on the size of the unit. Lift carefully and slide the stanchion brackets

(part of the upper track assembly) onto the top of the stanchions previously installed in the lower track assembly. Install the sway braces on the upper track with the hardware provided with the kit. Finger tighten only until the exact location is determined. Slide the sway braces out until they contact the wall. Level the center stanchions in both directions, keeping the ends of the sway braces against the wall, then tighten the sway brace bolts (see illustration next page).

Level the top of the unit by moving the sway braces up or down as necessary. Secure the braces to the wall with nails, wood screws, toggle bolts or wall anchors as required.

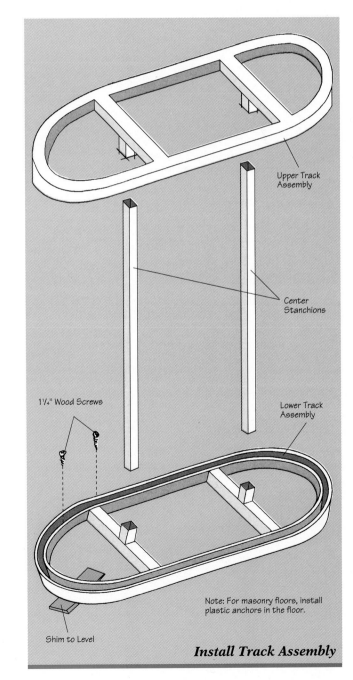

Upper Track Assembly

Center Stanchions

1¹/₄" Wood Screws

Lower Track Assembly

Note: For masonry floors, install plastic anchors in the floor.

Shim to Level

Install Track Assembly

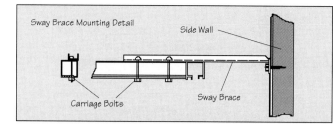

Sway Brace Mounting Detail
Side Wall
Carriage Bolts
Sway Brace

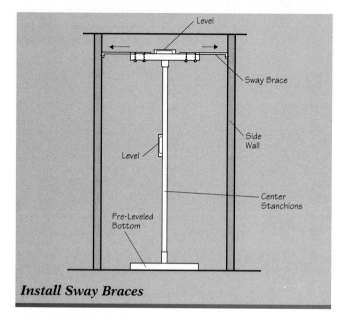

Install Sway Braces

Level
Sway Brace
Side Wall
Level
Center Stanchions
Pre-Leveled Bottom

4 *Install Switch*

CAUTION: *Depending on the type of unit, wiring may vary. Read the manufacturer's instructions thoroughly before making connections.*

The switch should be installed at normal switch height, close to the door so that the closet user can view the clothes going by while depressing the switch. Make a hole at the switch location so that the switch plate can be installed flush against the wall. Since the wire is only carrying signal voltage (24 volts AC) it can be surface mounted. Route the wire from the switch all the way through the wall.

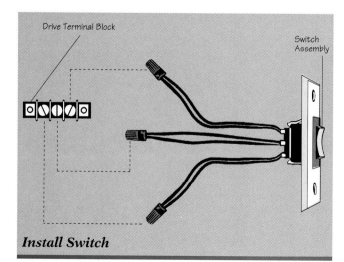

Drive Terminal Block
Switch Assembly

Install Switch

Connect the three-conductor 18-gauge wire and run to the terminal block on the drive unit. The center tap on the terminal block and switch are usually common. Check the wiring diagram for your unit. Make connections. Be sure all wire is secured and out of the way of the unit's operation.

5 *Install Lower Chain Assembly*

The lower conveyor chain is preassembled and consists of load bars and connecting links. Carefully unfold the lower chain assembly. Place it in the lower track and make the final screw connection. Use a pair of pliers to hold the roller shaft while the screw is being secured. The upper conveyor chain should be in place. Study this assembly if you have any problems installing the lower chain assembly.

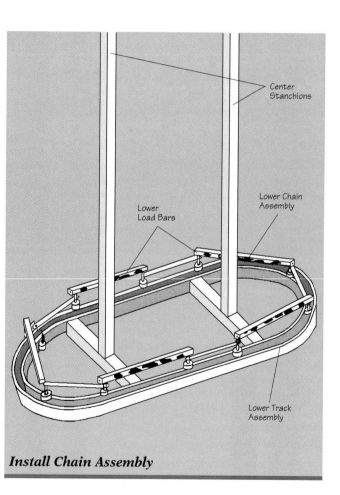

Center Stanchions
Lower Chain Assembly
Lower Load Bars
Lower Track Assembly

Install Chain Assembly

6 *Install Vertical Supports*

Set a vertical support in place. Secure to the end of the upper load bar with the screw provided. Install another support at the other end of the load bar, then two at each of the remaining load bars. After all the vertical supports are installed to the upper load bars, install to the lower load bars in the same manner (see illustration above and next page).

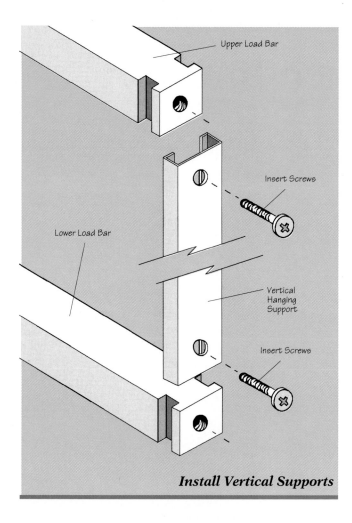

Install Vertical Supports

Upper Load Bar

Insert Screws

Lower Load Bar

Vertical Hanging Support

Insert Screws

8 Install Organizers

Install hanging rods into the vertical supports. There are two sets of holes, at the top and in the middle. Use both sets for double-hanging areas. Mounting hardware is provided with the revolving organizer kit.

Baskets and shoe racks may be installed at any location, and may be stacked at any desired spacing. Insert the spring nuts provided with the kit into the bin in the vertical supports. Rotate to a locking position with a screwdriver. Use two per side (four per basket). Set the basket into position. Insert the screws provided with the kit. Level the basket, and then tighten the screws.

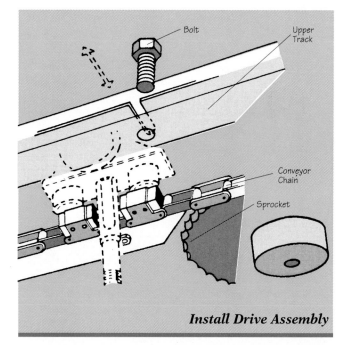

Bolt

Upper Track

Conveyor Chain

Sprocket

Install Drive Assembly

7 Install Drive Assembly

The drive assembly is a completely assembled unit that must be installed on the conveyor. Remove the sprocket cover by undoing the two screws. Partially thread the bolts into the threaded holes in the upper track. Lift the drive assembly and slide it toward the track with the slots engaging the studs. Make sure that one of the vertical pins on the conveyor chain is located between the two closely spaced pusher dogs on the drive chain. Be certain the drive base is tight against the upper track assembly; then tighten the bolts. Reinstall the sprocket cover.

Plug the unit into the appropriate outlet. Check the specifications provided with the unit. Before operating, check to be sure that all obstructions are out of the way and that the upper and lower tracks are free to move. All guide rollers should be in the tracks and should move freely. Make sure the power and signal wires are secured so that they are out of the way, and that all tools have been removed from the area. Turn on the switch. The unit should run smoothly and quietly. If you notice any jerking motions, or if scraping noises occur, check the upper and lower tracks for any foreign objects or bindings.

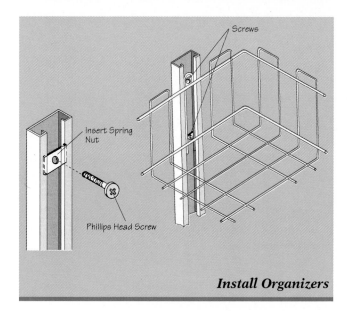

Screws

Insert Spring Nut

Phillips Head Screw

Install Organizers

Wall-to-Wall Reach-In Closet

Two spare feet at one end of a room is ample space to build a new closet. Of course, the wall must not contain any windows or doors. Properly organized, a wall-to-wall reach-in closet can meet your most demanding needs.

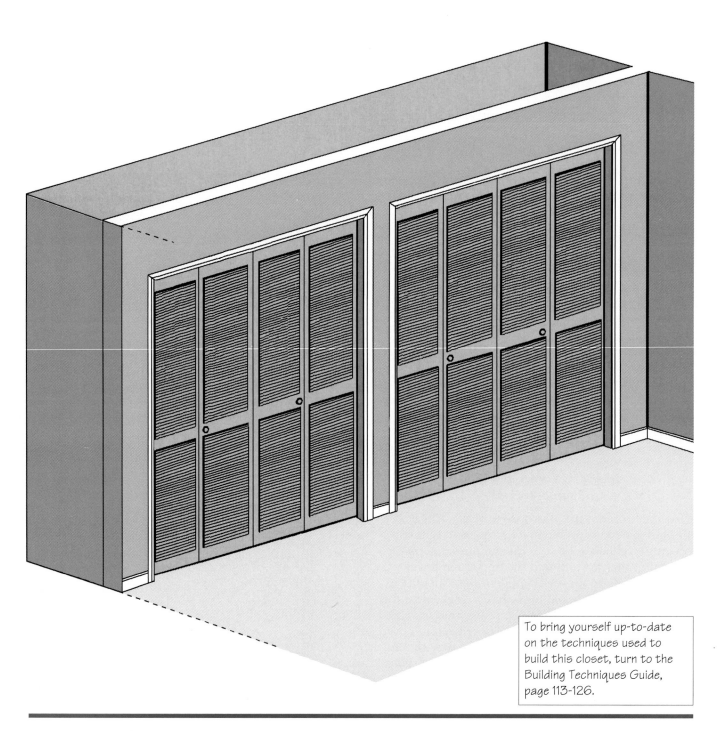

To bring yourself up-to-date on the techniques used to build this closet, turn to the Building Techniques Guide, page 113-126.

* Time required does not include drying time for joint compound.
* This project requires two workers.

Tools & Materials

- ☐ Magnetic Stud Finder
- ☐ Plumb Bob
- ☐ Combination Square
- ☐ Pencil
- ☐ Utility Knife
- ☐ Coping Saw
- ☐ 8d Nails
- ☐ 6d Finishing Nails
- ☐ Closet Doors
- ☐ 8' Baseboard
- ☐ (12) 2x4x8 (One door)
- ☐ Strips of 1/2"-Thick Material for Spacers
- ☐ Hammer
- ☐ Measuring Tape
- ☐ Framing Square
- ☐ Chalk Line
- ☐ Level
- ☐ Circular Saw
- ☐ 12d Nails
- ☐ 6-mil Polyethylene Sheeting
- ☐ Concrete Nails (Concrete slabs only)
- ☐ (2) 2x6x8
- ☐ (18) 2x4x8 (Two doors)

When Working with Gypsum Wallboard:
- ☐ 6" Drywall Knife
- ☐ 9" Drywall Knife
- ☐ Putty Knives (2" or smaller)

Item	Wall Length			
	6'-8'	8'-10'	10'-12'	12'-14'
☐ 2x4 for Bottom Plate (Pressure treated if on concrete slab)	8'	10'	12'	14'
☐ 2x4 for Top Plate	8'	10'	12'	14'
For Drywall:				
☐ 4x8 Drywall	4			
☐ 4x12 Sheets Drywall		4	4	5
☐ Drywall Nails				
☐ Drywall Tape				
☐ Drywall Joint Compound				
For Paneling:				
☐ 4x8 Sheets	4	5	6	7
☐ Crown Molding	16'	20'	24'	28'
☐ 48' Inside Corner Trim				
☐ Paneling Nails				
☐ 4d Finishing Nails				

For Cedar:
Compute the square footage to be covered. Allow 10%-20% extra for waste.

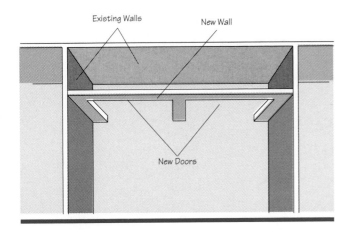

1 Locate Front Wall

For a 2'-deep closet, measure 24", then 27½" out from each end of the wall that is to become the back wall of the new closet. Mark these two measurements on the ceiling at each end. Snap a chalk line between the marks. This is the location of the new closet wall. Hold a plumb bob at the end of one line and mark the plumbed location on the floor. Repeat for the other line, then at the other ends of the lines. Snap lines on the floor at the marks.

Use the lines on the ceiling and floor as guides to snap chalk lines on the side walls to mark the locations where the new closet wall will connect to the existing walls. The lines on the side walls should be 1/2" outside the lines on the ceiling and floor. The additional space is needed to get a T assembly into the existing wall. Remove the wall finish material between the lines as detailed on page 118.

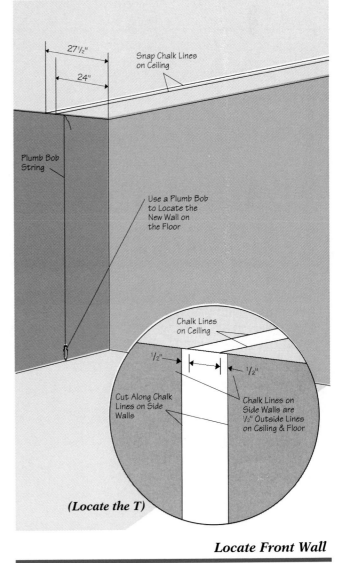

(Locate the T)

Locate Front Wall

2 Install a T in Each Side Wall

A T is an assembly of studs and blocking used to tie an intersecting wall into a straight wall. Build and install a T at the chalk lines snapped on each side wall as detailed on page 114.

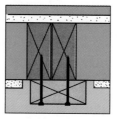

3 Cut Bottom Plate

At floor level, measure the distance between the side walls. Keep the tape measure between the chalk lines on the floor. Select a 2x4 that is slightly longer than the measured distance and mark the distance on the 2x4. This will be the bottom plate for the new wall. If the floor is concrete slab or other masonry material, the 2x4 should be pressure treated. Using a combination square, draw a perpendicular line through the mark and cut with a circular saw.

4 Mark Bottom Plate

Measure 1½" from one end of the bottom plate and use a combination square to draw a perpendicular line through the mark. Write an X between the line and the end of the bottom plate. Repeat at the other end. The Xs denote the location of the end studs. These studs are part of the T you installed in each of the existing side walls.

5 Mark Door Framing

Look in the prehung door chart (on the following page) under the width for your closet to find out how many and what size doors to use.

If you are using one door, locate the center of the wall and measure half the rough opening in each direction. Draw a line through the marks and place an X on the outside of each line. Measure another 1½" on each side, draw two more lines, and place two more Xs on the outside of the lines.

If you are using two doors, double the rough opening and subtract from the length of the wall. Divide the remainder by three. (The result, dimension A, must be at least 6". If not, use doors that are one size smaller.) Measure this remainder from one end of the bottom plate and draw a line. Place an X on the side of the line closest to the end you measured from. Starting from the line, measure the rough opening of the door. Draw a new line through this mark and place an X on the side nearest the center of the wall. At each of the two

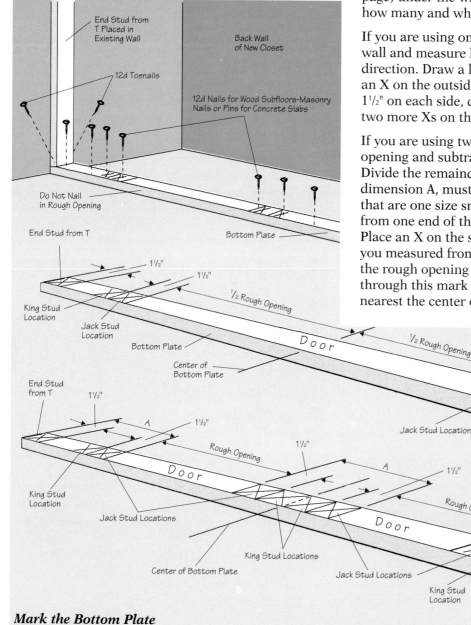

Mark the Bottom Plate

Time Required:	Novice	Average	Experienced
	4 Days	3 Days	1.5 Days

* Time required does not include drying time for joint compound.

* This project requires two workers.

Tools & Materials List

☐ Hammer   ☐ Plumb Bob

☐ Measuring Tape   ☐ Combination Square

☐ Framing Square   ☐ Pencil

☐ Chalk Line   ☐ Utility Knife

☐ Circular Saw   ☐ Level

☐ Coping Saw   ☐ Miter Saw

☐ Crosscut (Hand) Saw   ☐ 8d nails

☐ 12d Nails   ☐ Concrete Nails (Concrete slabs only)

☐ 6d Finishing Nails   ☐ Plastic Film (Protect flooring)

☐ Closet Doors   ☐ 12' Baseboard

☐ (2) 2x6x8   ☐ (16) 2x4x8 (One door)

☐ (22) 2x4x8 (Two doors)

☐ Strips of 1/2"-Thick Material for Spacers

When Working with Gypsum Wallboard:

☐ 6" Putty Knife   ☐ 9" Putty Knife

	Closet Width		
Item	**4'-6'**	**6'-8'**	**8'-10'**
☐ 2x4 for Bottom Plate (Pressure treated if on concrete slab)	8'	10'	12'
☐ 2x4 for Top Plate	8'	10'	12'
For Drywall:			
☐ 4x8 Sheets Drywall	4	5	
☐ 4x12 Sheets Drywall			4
☐ Drywall Nails			
☐ Drywall Tape			
☐ 8' Metal Corner			
☐ Gypsum Compound			
☐ Drywall Joint Compound			
For Paneling:			
☐ 4x8 Sheets	4	5	6
☐ Crown Molding	16'	20'	24'
☐ 48' Inside Corner Trim			
☐ 8' Outside Corner Trim			
☐ Paneling Nails			
☐ 4d Finishing Nails			

For Cedar:

Compute the square footage to be covered. Allow 10%-20% extra for waste.

1 Locate Closet Front Wall

For a 2'-deep closet, measure 24", then 27½" out from the wall that will become the back wall of the new closet. This should be done at each side of the new closet. Mark the measurements on the ceiling, then snap chalk lines between the marks. From the side wall, measure the new closet width and mark it on the ceiling. Add 3½" and make

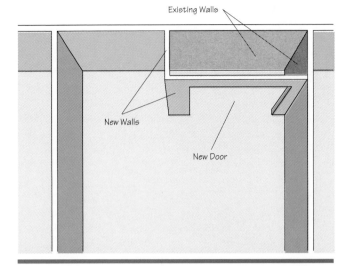

Existing Walls

New Walls

New Door

another mark. Use a pencil and framing square to draw the side wall of the new closet on the ceiling.

Hold a plumb bob at one end of the line for the front wall of the closet and mark the plumbed location on the floor (see illustration next page). Repeat for the other line, then for the other end of each line. Snap lines on the floor at the marks. Hold the plumb bob at one end of the new closet side wall and mark on the floor. Then, mark the other line. Use a framing square to draw the side wall lines on the floor.

Use the lines on the ceiling and floor as guides to snap chalk lines on the side wall and back wall to mark the locations where the closet will connect to the existing walls. The lines on the side walls should be 1/2" outside the lines on the ceiling and floor (see illustration next page). The additional space is needed to frame a T into the existing wall. Remove the wall finish material between the lines as detailed on page 118.

2 Install a T in Existing Walls

Build and install a T at the chalk lines snapped on the side and back existing walls as detailed on page 114.

3 Cut Bottom Plate

At floor level, measure the distance from the existing side wall to the far line of the closet side wall. Keep the tape measure between the chalk lines on the floor. Select a 2x4 that is at least 24" longer than the measured distance and mark the distance on the 2x4. This will be the bottom plate for the front wall (see illustration next page). If you are securing the plate to a concrete slab or other masonry material, use pressure-treated lumber.

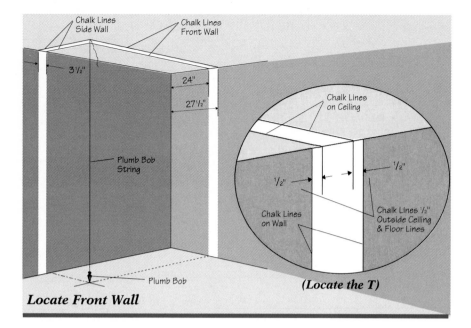

Locate Front Wall

(Locate the T)

Using a combination square, draw a perpendicular line through the mark and cut with a circular saw. From the remaining piece, cut another piece to 24" long. This is the bottom plate for the closet side wall.

NOTE: *Use 12d nails for wood subfloors, masonry nails or pins for concrete slabs.*

4 *Mark Side Wall*

Measure 1½" from one end of the side wall bottom plate and mark the location of the first wall stud, drawing a perpendicular line through the mark. Write an X between the line and the end of the bottom plate. Repeat at the other end. Measure 12¾" from either end to locate the remaining stud. Write an X on the side of the line closest to the end from which you measured. The Xs denote which side of the line the studs belong.

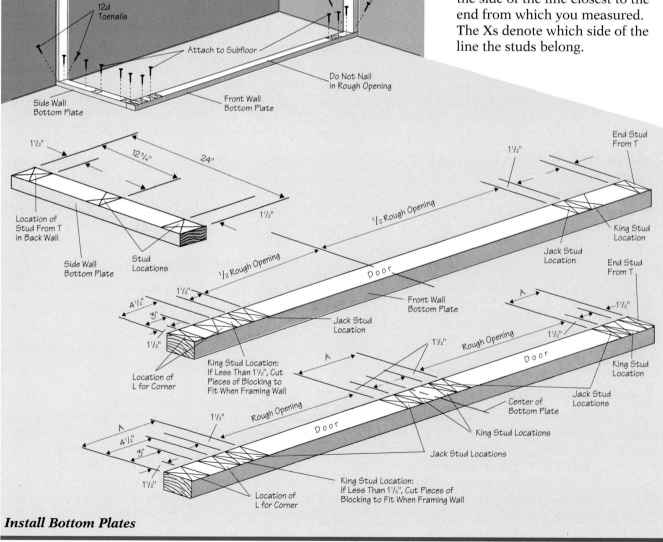

Install Bottom Plates

5 Mark Bottom Plate

Measure 1½" from one end of the front wall bottom plate and draw a line through the mark. Write an X between the line and the end of the bottom plate. At the other end, measure 1½" and 4½". Draw an X at each line, on the side closest to the end from which you measured.

6 Mark Door Framing

Refer to the chart below to determine how many and what size prehung doors to use:

Nearest Closet Width	Number Of Doors	Size Of Doors	Rough Opening Each Door
3'	1	2' 6"	33"
4'	1	3' 0"	39"
5'	1	4' 0"	51"
6'	1	5' 0"	63"
7'	1	6' 0"	75"
8'-9'	2	3' 0"	39"
10'	2	4' 0"	51"

If you are installing one door, locate the center of the front wall and measure half the rough opening in each direction. (There should be a minimum of 6" from the mark to the end of the bottom plate at each end. If not, use a door that is one size smaller.) Draw a line through the marks and place an X on the outside of each line. Measure another 1½" on each side, draw two more lines, and place two more Xs on the outside of the lines.

If you are installing two doors, double the rough opening and subtract from the length of the wall. Divide the remainder by three. (The result, dimension A, must be at least 6". If not, use doors that are one size smaller.) Measure this remainder from one end of the bottom plate and draw a line. Place an X on the side of the line closest to the end from which you measured. Next, measure the rough opening of the door from the line. Draw a new line through this mark and place an X on the side nearest the center of the wall. At each of the two lines, measure 1½" away from the rough opening. Draw two new lines and place another X at each, both on the side away from the rough opening. Repeat the entire process at the other end of the bottom plate. Check your work by measuring the three areas that are not part of the rough openings. They should all be the same length.

Regardless of how many doors you will use, the first X beyond the rough opening on each side denotes the location of the shorter "jack" stud and the second X denotes the location of a full-length "king" stud.

NOTE: *The term stud in this case does not mean a precut stud. If you have a standard 8' ceiling, a full-length stud in the new wall will be slightly longer than a precut stud since we are only using one top plate.*

If the distance from the edge of the rough opening to the end of the bottom plate that intersects the new side wall is less than 7½", there will not be enough room for a king stud on the end where the two new walls will meet. So you will need to rip pieces of blocking to fit between the jack stud and end stud when framing the walls.

If there is more than 16" between full-length studs at any point in the wall other than the rough openings, additional studs will need to be added at 16" on center. Start measuring at one end and draw a line at 16¾". Write an X on the side of the line closest to the end from which you started measuring to denote the stud locations. Continue measuring in 16" increments until you reach the other end of the plate. Do not place marks in the door rough openings.

7 Cut & Mark Top Plates

At ceiling level, measure the distance from the existing side wall to the far line of the closet side wall. Keep the measuring tape between the chalk lines. (Since few houses are perfectly square, you cannot use the measurement made on the floor.) Select a 2x4 that is at least 24" longer than the measured distance, then cut to fit. This will be the top plate for the front wall. From the remaining piece, cut another piece to 24" long. This is the top plate for the closet side wall. Lay the front wall top plate side-by-side with the front wall bottom plate. If there is a variation in the length, center the plates with each other. (The end studs, however, will still be measured and marked at 1½" from the ends of the top plate.) Use a combination square to project the lines from the bottom plate onto the top plate. Draw an X at each line as was done on the bottom plate. Repeat for the side wall top plate.

8 Install Bottom & Top Plates

See the drawings on the previous and next pages and refer to page 113 for instructions on installing the bottom plates, then follow instructions for installing the top plates.

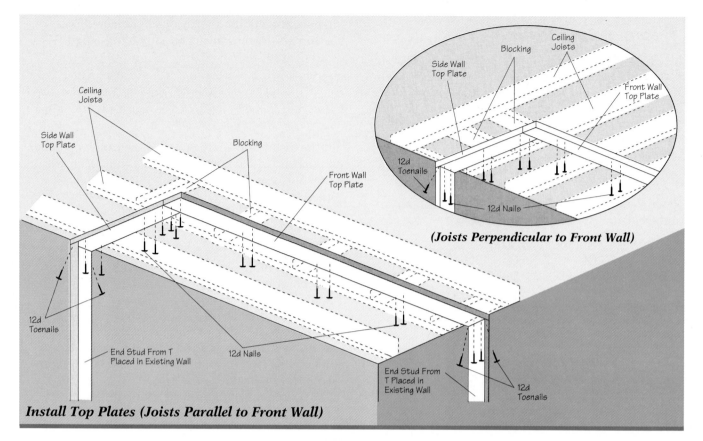

Ceiling Joists

Side Wall Top Plate

Blocking

Front Wall Top Plate

12d Toenails

End Stud From T Placed in Existing Wall

12d Nails

Install Top Plates (Joists Parallel to Front Wall)

End Stud From T Placed in Existing Wall

12d Toenails

Blocking

Ceiling Joists

Side Wall Top Plate

Front Wall Top Plate

12d Toenails

12d Nails

(Joists Perpendicular to Front Wall)

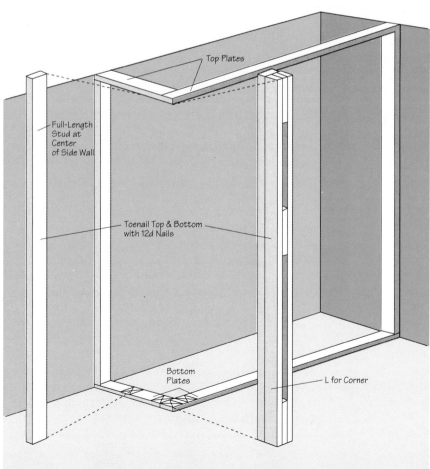

Top Plates

Full-Length Stud at Center of Side Wall

Toenail Top & Bottom with 12d Nails

Bottom Plates

L for Corner

Build an L & Install Studs (Side Wall)

9 *Build an L*

An L is needed at the corner formed by the intersection of the two new walls. See page 115 for the construction of an L. Set the L in place on the marks. The long side of the L goes in the front wall. Toenail each side of the three studs in the L into the bottom and top plates with 12d nails (see illustration next page).

10 *Install Studs*

Measure the length of the stud in the center of the side wall and cut a 2x4 to fit. Studs should be cut to the precise length, so measure carefully from the top surface of the bottom plate to the bottom surface of the top plate. Set the cut stud into place and test for fit. If it is too long, do not force it into place. Trim as needed. If it is a little too short, shim to fit. If it is substantially too short, cut a new stud. Toenail the stud into place with 12d nails, two top and two bottom.

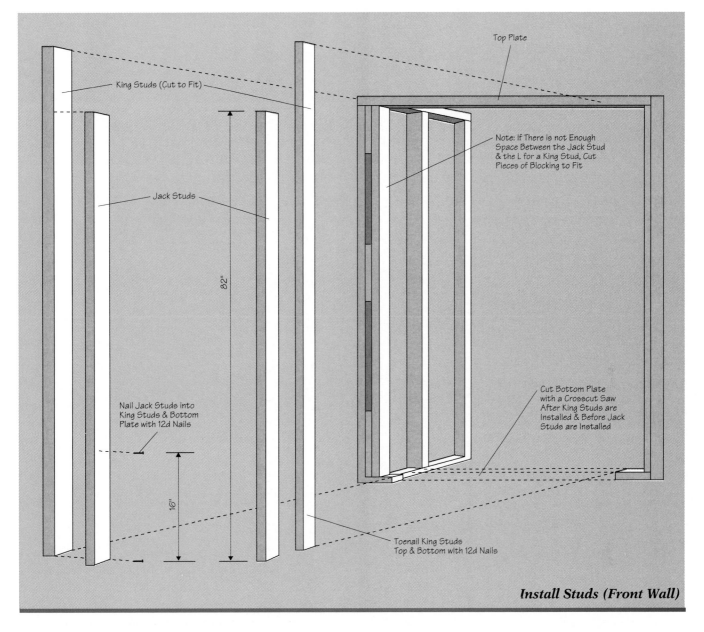

Install Studs (Front Wall)

Labels in figure:
- King Studs (Cut to Fit)
- Jack Studs
- Top Plate
- 82"
- 16"
- Nail Jack Studs into King Studs & Bottom Plate with 12d Nails
- Note: If There is not Enough Space Between the Jack Stud & the L for a King Stud, Cut Pieces of Blocking to Fit
- Cut Bottom Plate with a Crosscut Saw After King Studs are Installed & Before Jack Studs are Installed
- Toenail King Studs Top & Bottom with 12d Nails

Start at one end of the front wall and measure the length of the first full-length stud. This will probably be a king stud for a door. Toenail the stud into the top and bottom plates with 12d nails as before. Continue until all full-length studs are installed.

Use a crosscut saw to cut and remove the bottom plate in the area of the rough opening. Cut two 2x4s to 82" long each. (This is for a standard 6' 8" high door. If you are using a nonstandard door, consult the manufacturer's directions.) Set the jack studs in place against the king studs. The bottom of the jack studs will rest on the floor. Nail each jack stud into the bottom plate with two 12d nails. Nail into the king studs approximately every 16" with 12d nails. Use two nails at the top of each jack stud. Repeat for a second door.

11 Construct & Install Door Header

See page 119 for instructions on constructing and installing the door header.

12 Install Cripples (Above Header)

See page 119 for instructions on installing the cripple studs.

13 Install Finish Materials

Install the finish wall materials of your choice on the inside and outside walls of the closet. Next, install closet organizer, closet doors, baseboard and trim. Finally, install the carpet, if any. See pages 121-126.

Basic Walk-In Closet

A walk-in closet, unlike a reach-in, requires a minimum width of 6 feet and a minimum depth of 5 feet (6 feet preferred). Since there may not be enough space to add a walk-in to your bedroom, it might be easier to convert an existing reach-in closet. This will take less square footage out of the bedroom.

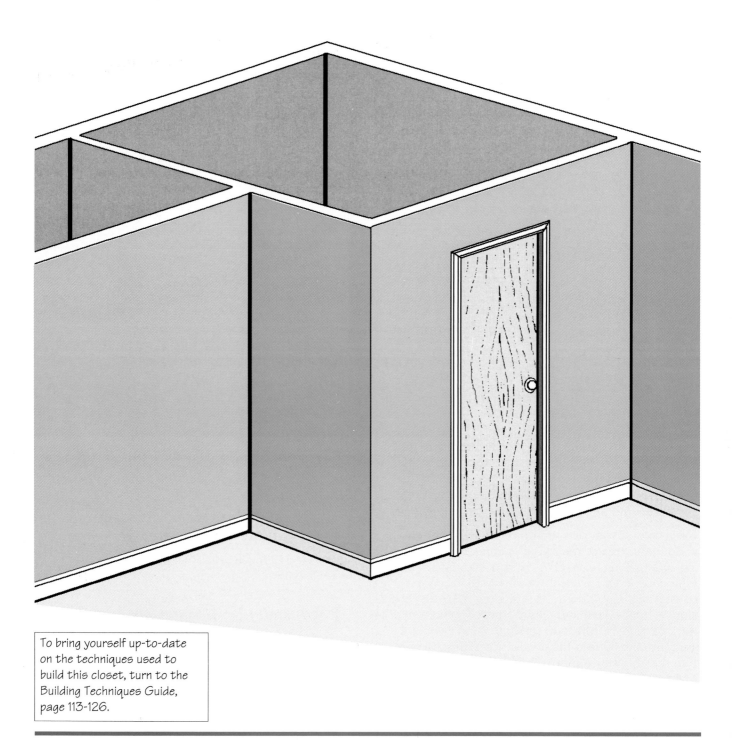

To bring yourself up-to-date on the techniques used to build this closet, turn to the Building Techniques Guide, page 113-126.

Time Required:	Novice	Average	Experienced
Wall Removal (If Necessary)	1 Day	1 Day	.5 Day
Construction	4 Days	3 Days	1.5 Days

* Does not include drying time for joint compound.
* This project requires two workers.

NOTE: *The material list is based on a 6'x6' walk-in closet.*

Tools & Materials

- ☐ Hammer
- ☐ Measuring Tape
- ☐ Framing Square
- ☐ Chalk Line
- ☐ Circular Saw
- ☐ Coping Saw
- ☐ Crosscut (Hand) Saw
- ☐ 12d Nails
- ☐ 6d Finishing Nails
- ☐ 2068 Door
- ☐ (2) 2x6x8
- ☐ (1) 2x4x14 (Pressure treated if concrete slab)
- ☐ 24' Baseboard
- ☐ Strip of 1/2"-Thick Material (For spacer for door header)

- ☐ Plumb Bob
- ☐ Combination Square
- ☐ Pencil
- ☐ Utility Knife
- ☐ Level
- ☐ Miter Saw
- ☐ 8d Nails
- ☐ Concrete Nails (Concrete slabs only)
- ☐ Plastic Film (Protect flooring)
- ☐ (20) 2x4x8
- ☐ (1) 2x4x14

When Working with Gypsum Wallboard:
- ☐ 6" and 9" Putty Knives

For Drywall:
- ☐ (8) 4x8 Sheets Drywall
- ☐ Drywall Tape
- ☐ Gypsum Compound
- ☐ Drywall Nails
- ☐ 8' Metal Corner

For Paneling:
- ☐ (7) 4x8 Sheets
- ☐ 48' Inside Corner Trim
- ☐ Paneling Nails
- ☐ 24' Crown Molding
- ☐ 8' Outside Corner Trim
- ☐ 4d Finishing Nails

For Cedar Interior:
Compute the square footage to be covered.
Allow 10%-20% for waste.

1 *Remove an Existing Wall*

If you are going to convert an existing reach-in closet, the first step will be to remove the existing closet front wall. However, before removal you must check to be sure the wall is not a bearing wall. Refer to page 117, to determine if a wall is bearing, and for the additional steps required if it is. Then, follow the guidelines on page 118 for removing the wall.

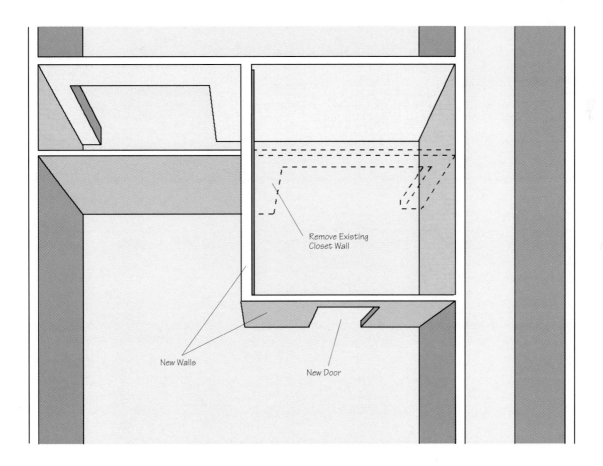

Remove Existing Closet Wall

New Walls

New Door

2 Locate New Walls

Starting in the corner where the closet will be located, measure 72" and 75½" in each direction (these measurements are based on a closet with a depth of 6'—adjust for deeper closets) and place marks on the ceiling. From each mark measure 72" and 75½" perpendicular to the wall from which you are measuring and place marks on the ceiling.

Hold a plumb bob at one end of the line for the front wall of the closet and mark the plumbed location on the floor. Repeat for the other line, then for the other end of each line. Snap lines on the floor at the marks. Use the plumb bob to locate the side wall on the floor in the same manner.

Use the lines on the ceiling and floor as guides to snap chalk lines on the side wall and back wall to mark the locations where the closet will connect to the existing walls. The lines on the walls should be 1/2" outside the lines on the ceiling and floor (inset). The additional space is needed to get a T into the existing wall. Remove the wall finish material between the lines as detailed on page 118.

3 Install a T in the Existing Walls

A T is an assembly of studs and blocking used to firmly tie an intersecting wall into a straight wall. Build and install a T at the chalk lines snapped on the side and back existing walls as detailed on page 114.

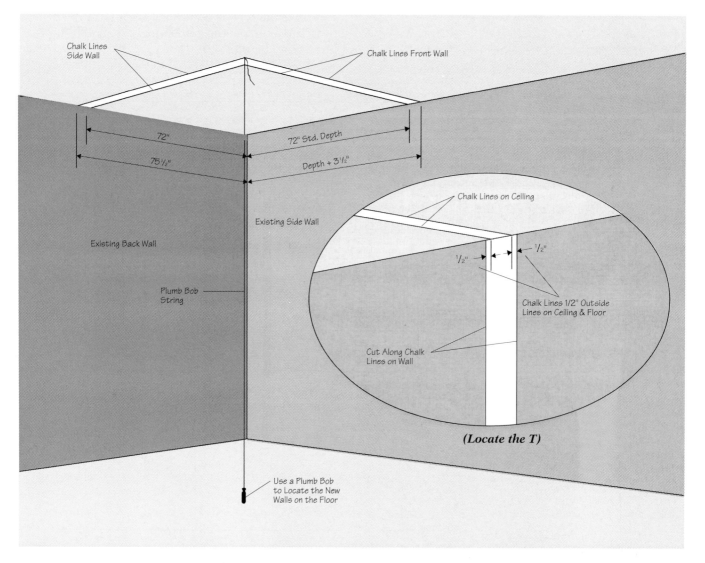

(Locate the T)

Locate New Walls

4 Cut & Mark Bottom Plates

At floor level, measure the distance from the existing side wall to the far line of the closet side wall and cut a 2x4 bottom plate to this length. This is the front wall bottom plate. Repeat the process for the side wall bottom plate, taking your measurement from the back wall to the inside edge of the new front wall. Mark the stud locations on the bottom plates (including locations of jack studs and king studs on front plate).

5 Cut & Mark Top Plates

At ceiling level, measure the distance from the existing side wall to the far line of the new closet side wall. It should be 75½" as originally marked. Cut a 2x4 top plate to this length. Then, measure and cut the top plate for the side wall. The measurement should be made from the back wall to the inside edge of the new front wall and should be 72".

Lay the front wall top plate side-by-side with the front wall bottom plate. If there is a variation in the length, center the plates with each other. (The end studs, however, will still be measured and marked at 1½" from the ends of the top plate.) Then project the stud location lines from the bottom plate onto the top plate. Repeat for the side wall top plate.

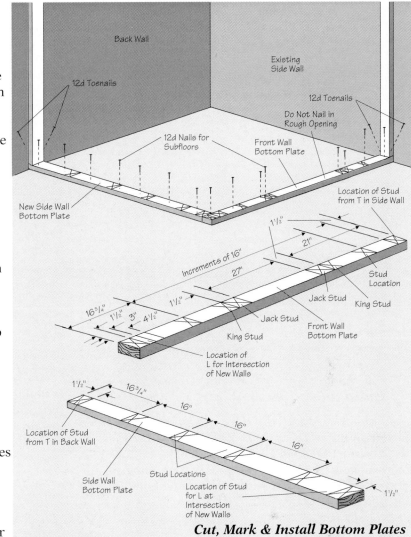

Cut, Mark & Install Bottom Plates

6 Install Top & Bottom Plates

See the drawings on this page and refer to pages 87 and 113 for detailed instruction.

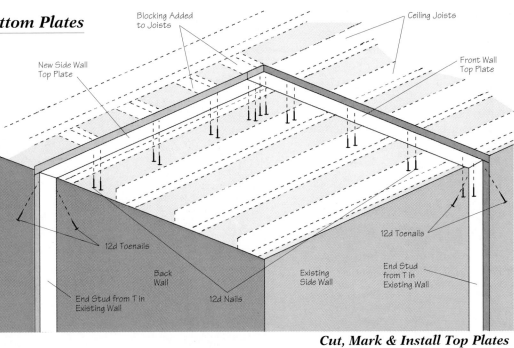

Cut, Mark & Install Top Plates

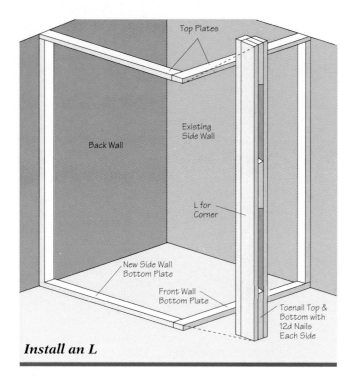

Install an L

7 Build an L

An L is needed at the corner formed by the intersection of the two new walls. Refer to page 115 for the construction of an L. Set the L in place on the marks. The long side of the L goes in the front wall. Toenail each side of the three studs in the L into the top and bottom plates with 12d nails.

8 Install Studs

Measure the length of the first stud at either end of the new side wall and cut a 2x4 to fit. Studs should be cut to the precise length, so measure carefully from the top surface of the bottom plate to the bottom surface of the top plate. Set the cut stud into place and test for fit. If it is too long, do not force it into place. Trim as needed. If it is a little too short, shim to fit. If it is substantially too short, cut a new stud. Toenail the stud into place with 12d nails, two top and two bottom. Continue until all side wall studs are installed. Start at either end of the front wall and measure the length of the first full-length stud. Toenail the stud into the top and bottom plates with 12d nails as before. Continue until all full-length studs are installed.

Use a crosscut saw to cut and remove the bottom plate in the area of the rough opening. Cut two 2x4 jack studs to 82" long. (This is for a standard 6' 8" high door. If you are using a nonstandard door, consult the manufacturer's directions.) Set the jack studs in place against the king studs. The bottom of the jack studs will rest on the floor. Nail each jack stud into the bottom plate with two 12d nails. Nail into the king studs approximately every 16" with 12d nails. Use two nails at the top of each jack stud. Repeat for a second door.

9 Construct & Install Header & Cripples

See page 119 for instructions on installing the header and cripples.

10 Install Cripples (Above Header)

See page 119 for instructions on installing the cripple studs.

11 Install Finish Materials

Install the finish wall materials of your choice on the inside and outside walls of the closet. Next, install closet organizers, closet doors, baseboard and other trim. Finally, install the carpet, if any (see page 121-126.).

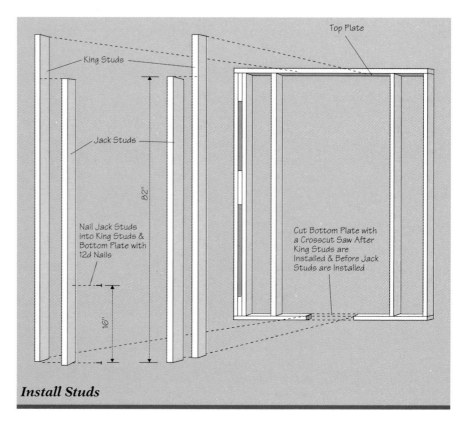

Install Studs

His & Her Walk-In Closets

Two small bedrooms can be transformed into one large bedroom with his and her walk-in closets. Well-organized closets eliminate clutter and leave the bedroom spacious and comfortable.

This idea is perfect for families with children that have grown up, moved out of the house and left their rooms empty.

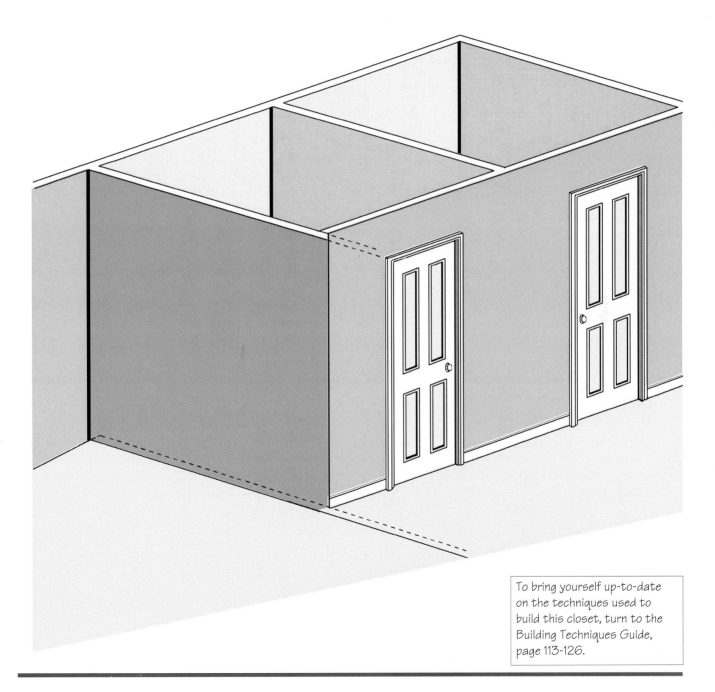

To bring yourself up-to-date on the techniques used to build this closet, turn to the Building Techniques Guide, page 113-126.

* Time required does not include drying time for joint compound.
* This project requires two workers.

Tools & Materials

☐ Plumb Bob	☐ Measuring Tape
☐ Combination Square	☐ Framing Square
☐ Pencil	☐ Chalk Line
☐ Utility Knife	☐ Circular Saw
☐ Level	☐ Coping Saw
☐ Miter Saw	☐ Crosscut (Hand) Saw
☐ Crowbar	☐ 8d Nails
☐ 12d Nails	☐ 6d Finishing Nails
☐ Plastic Film (Protect flooring)	☐ (2) 2068 Doors
☐ (26-32) 2x4x8	☐ (3) 2x6x8
☐ (1) 2x4x(Wall Length)	☐ 26'-38' Baseboard

☐ Masonry Chisel (If walls are lath and plaster)
☐ Concrete Nails (Concrete slabs only)
☐ Strips of 1/2"-Thick Material (For spacers for door header)
☐ (1) 2x4x(Wall Length) (Pressure treated if concrete slab)
☐ (1) 2x4x8 (Pressure treated if concrete slab)

When Working with Wallboard:
☐ 6" and 9" Putty Knife

For Drywall:

☐ (8) 4x12 Sheets Drywall	☐ Drywall Nails
☐ Drywall Tape	☐ Gypsum Compound

For Paneling:

☐ (12) 4x8 Sheets	☐ 34'-46' Crown Molding
☐ 80' Inside Corner Trim	☐ Paneling Nails
☐ 4d Finishing Nails	

For Cedar:

Compute the square footage to be covered.
Add 10%–20% for waste.

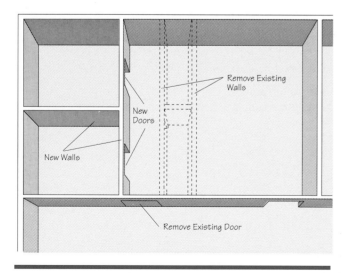

1 *Remove Existing Walls*

Two small bedrooms may be separated by a simple partition or by reach-in closets. Either way, the existing wall (or walls) will have to be removed. Before removal, however, you must check to be sure the wall is not a bearing (or load-carrying) wall. If the two bedrooms are perpendicular to the length of the house, it is likely that the dividing wall is a bearing wall. If the bedrooms are parallel to the length of the house, it is less likely but still possible. A trip into the attic will determine whether or not the wall is load bearing, if so you must add a beam. Then remove the wall finish materials (see pages 117-118).

2 *Locate New Walls*

Decide which wall you want to use for the closets. A width of 12' 4" feet is ideal, but it can vary from 11'4" to 16'4". If the width is less than 11'4", consider building one full walk-in closet and one half walk-in. For widths over 16'4" building two walk-in closets becomes an inefficient use of space.

For a closet which has a depth of 7', measure 84", then 87½" (adjust measurements for deeper closets) out from each end of the wall that will become the back wall of the new closets. Mark the measurements on the ceiling. Snap chalk lines between the marks. Subtract 3½" from the length of the back wall and divide the remainder by two. The result is the width of each of the new closets. Measure and mark this width from one of the side walls at the front and back of the closet. Measure an additional 3½" and place more marks. Snap chalk lines between the marks. The lines represent the dividing wall for the two closets.

Hold a plumb bob at one end of the line for the front wall of the closet and mark the plumbed location on the floor. Repeat for the other line, then for the other end of each line. Snap lines on the floor at the marks. Use the plumb bob to locate the dividing wall on the floor in the same manner.

Use the lines on the ceiling and floor as guides to snap chalk lines on the side walls and back wall to mark the locations where the closet walls will connect to the existing walls. The lines on the existing walls should be 1/2" outside the lines on the ceiling and floor. This additional space is needed to get a T into the existing wall. Remove the wall finish material between the lines as detailed on page 118.

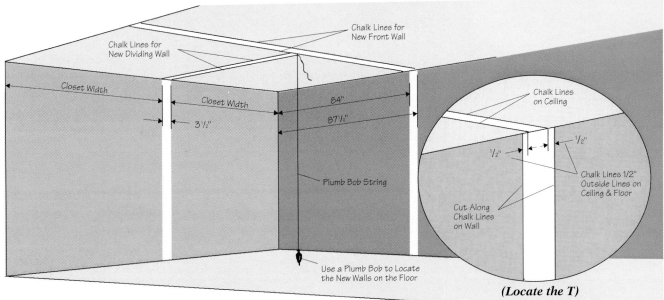

Chalk Lines for
New Front Wall

Chalk Lines for
New Dividing Wall

Closet Width

Closet Width

84"

87½"

3½"

Plumb Bob String

Use a Plumb Bob to Locate
the New Walls on the Floor

Chalk Lines
on Ceiling

½"

½"

Chalk Lines ½"
Outside Lines on
Ceiling & Floor

Cut Along
Chalk Lines
on Wall

(Locate the T)

Locate New Walls

3 *Install a T in Existing Walls*

A T is an assembly of lumber used to firmly tie an intersecting wall into a straight wall. Build and install a T at the chalk lines snapped on the side and back existing walls as detailed on page 114.

4 *Cut & Mark Bottom Plates*

At floor level, measure the length of the closet front wall, and cut the bottom plate to fit. (Since few houses are perfectly square, you cannot use the length of the back wall.) Keep the tape measure between the chalk lines on the floor.

Select a 2x4 that is slightly longer than the measured distance and mark the distance on the 2x4. This will be the bottom plate for the new wall. If the floor is concrete slab or other masonry material, the 2x4 should be pressure treated. Using a combination square, draw a perpendicular line through the mark and cut with a circular saw.

Repeat the process for the dividing wall bottom plate. Measure from the back wall to the inside edge of the new front wall. Mark the stud locations on the bottom plates for the front wall and dividing walls (see illustration next page).

5 *Cut & Mark Top Plates*

At ceiling level, measure the length of the front wall. Keep the tape measure between the chalk lines. Cut a 2x4 top plate to this length. Then, measure and cut the top plate for the dividing wall. The measurement should be made from the back wall to the inside edge of the new front wall.

Lay the front wall top plate side-by-side with the front wall bottom plate. If there is a variation in the length, center the plates with each other. (The end studs, however, will still be measured and marked at 1½" from the ends of the top plate.) Project the lines from the bottom plate onto the top plate. Draw an X at each line as was done on the bottom plate. Repeat for the dividing wall top plate (see illustration next page).

6 *Install Plates*

Set the front wall bottom plate in place, carefully aligned between the chalk lines on the floor. Nail the plate to the floor using 12d nails for wood subfloors, masonry nails or pins for concrete slabs. Then toenail the end studs on the Ts previously placed into the existing side walls into the bottom plate. Do not nail the plate within the door opening. Refer to page 113 for details on toenailing. Repeat the process for the bottom plate of the dividing wall (except that there is no door opening).

Before nailing the top plates into place, you must determine which way the ceiling joists are running. Blocking will be required for either the front or divider wall. See page 116 for details on how to determine joist direction and how to install blocking.

Set the top plates in place, carefully aligned between the chalk lines, and nail into the ceiling joists or blocking with 12d nails, two each joist. Then toenail the end studs from the Ts placed in the existing walls to the top plates. Use one toenail each side of each T (see illustrations next page).

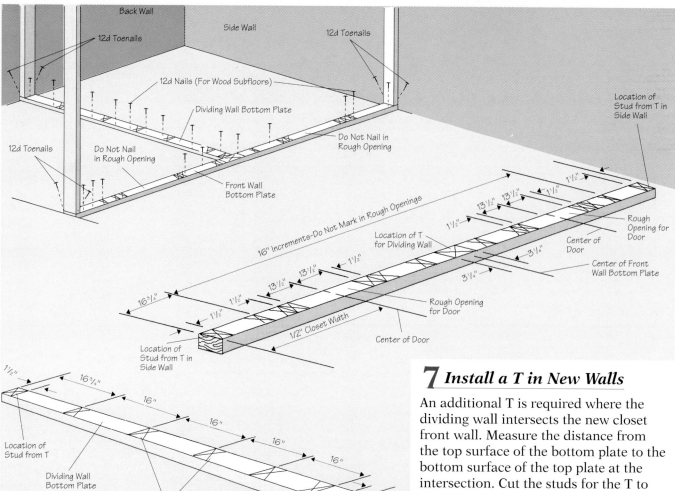

Cut, Mark & Install Bottom Plates

7 Install a T in New Walls

An additional T is required where the dividing wall intersects the new closet front wall. Measure the distance from the top surface of the bottom plate to the bottom surface of the top plate at the intersection. Cut the studs for the T to this dimension. Build the T as instructed on page 115. Set into place and toenail into the top and bottom plates with 12d nails, two at each end of each stud.

8 Install Studs

Starting at either end of the front wall, measure the length of the first stud and cut a 2x4 to fit. Toenail the stud into place with 12d nails, two top and two bottom. Repeat until you reach the other end of the wall, then repeat for the dividing wall.

Remove the bottom plate in the area of the rough openings. Cut four 2x4 jack studs to 82" long. (This length is for a standard 6' 8" high door. If you are using a nonstandard door, consult the manufacturer's directions.) The bottom of the jack studs will rest on the floor. Nail each jack stud into the bottom plate with two 12d nails, then into the king studs approximately every 16" with 12d nails. Use two nails at the top of each jack stud. Repeat for a second door (see illustration next page).

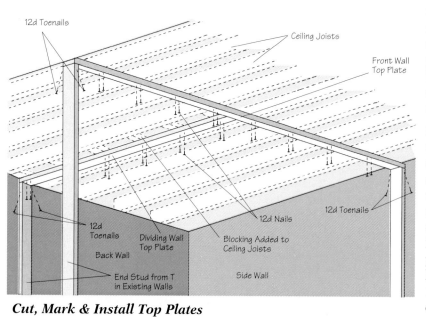

Cut, Mark & Install Top Plates

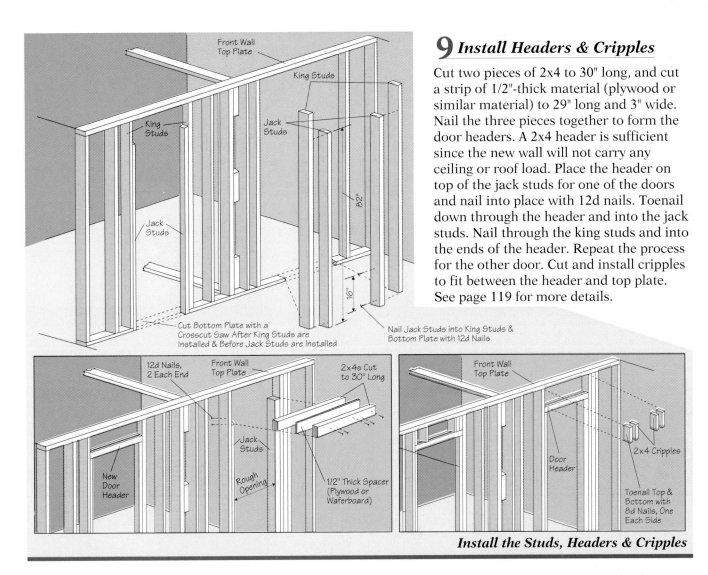

9 Install Headers & Cripples

Cut two pieces of 2x4 to 30" long, and cut a strip of 1/2"-thick material (plywood or similar material) to 29" long and 3" wide. Nail the three pieces together to form the door headers. A 2x4 header is sufficient since the new wall will not carry any ceiling or roof load. Place the header on top of the jack studs for one of the doors and nail into place with 12d nails. Toenail down through the header and into the jack studs. Nail through the king studs and into the ends of the header. Repeat the process for the other door. Cut and install cripples to fit between the header and top plate. See page 119 for more details.

Install the Studs, Headers & Cripples

10 Remove Extra Door

Since you are converting two rooms into one, there will be one too many entrance doors. Decide which door to remove, then take the door out of the frame. Pry the trim away from the door jamb all the way around. Use a crowbar and a piece of plywood as a backing so that you do not destroy the existing walls. Measure the width of the opening at the top and again at the bottom. Cut two lengths of 2x4 to fit. Measure the height of the opening on each side and in the middle and subtract 3". Cut three studs to this length. Nail the stud framework together with 12d nails, two each end of each stud. Slide this assembly into place and nail to the existing framing with 12d nails every 16".

11 Install Finish Materials

Install the finish wall materials of your choice on the inside and outside walls of the closet. Next, install closet organizer, closet doors, baseboard and trim. Finally, install the carpet, if any. See pages 121-126.

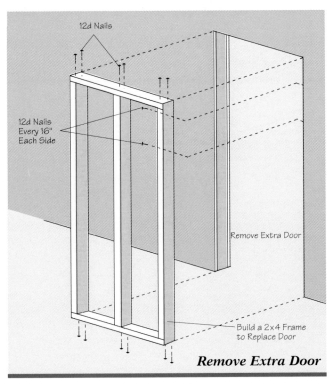

Remove Extra Door

Walk-In Closet & Dressing Room

A combination dressing area and walk-in closet built adjacent to the master bath is a luxury. If possible, some of the space lost to the new area may be reclaimed by converting the old closet to bedroom space.

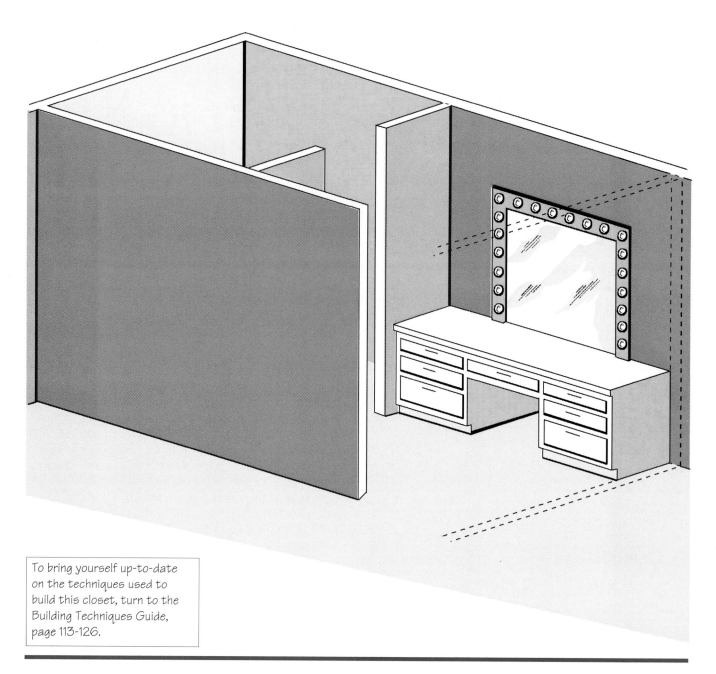

To bring yourself up-to-date on the techniques used to build this closet, turn to the Building Techniques Guide, page 113-126.

* Time required does not include drying time for joint compound.
* This project requires two workers.

NOTE: *The material list is based on a maximum bedroom width of 14' 4".*

Tools & Materials

- ☐ Hammer
- ☐ Measuring Tape
- ☐ Framing Square
- ☐ Chalk Line
- ☐ Circular Saw
- ☐ Coping Saw
- ☐ Crosscut (Hand) Saw
- ☐ 8d Nails
- ☐ 6d Finishing Nails
- ☐ Wood Screws for Vanity Top
- ☐ 6'-Wide Vanity
- ☐ Tub or Tile Sealant
- ☐ Full-Length Mirrors
- ☐ (2) 2x6x8
- ☐ Plumb Bob
- ☐ Combination Square
- ☐ Pencil
- ☐ Utility Knife
- ☐ Level
- ☐ Miter Saw
- ☐ Drill with Screwdriver Bits
- ☐ 12d Nails
- ☐ (6) #10x2¹/₂" Wood Screws
- ☐ Plastic Film (Protect flooring)
- ☐ 6'-Wide Vanity Top
- ☐ Make-Up Mirror with Lights
- ☐ (30) 2x4x8
- ☐ (1) 2x4x12
- ☐ Concrete Nails (Concrete slabs only)
- ☐ (1) 2x4x12 Pressure Treated (If concrete slab)
- ☐ (1) 2x4x8 Pressure Treated (If concrete slab)
- ☐ 32' Baseboard

When Working with Wallboard:
- ☐ 6" and 9" Putty Knife

For Drywall:
- ☐ (6) 4x8 Sheets Drywall
- ☐ 48' Metal Corner
- ☐ Drywall Tape
- ☐ (2) 4x12 Sheets Drywall
- ☐ Drywall Nails
- ☐ Joint Compound

For Paneling:
- ☐ (9) 4x8 Sheets
- ☐ 50' Inside Corner Trim
- ☐ Paneling Nails
- ☐ 32' Crown Molding
- ☐ 48' Outside Corner Trim
- ☐ 4d Finishing Nails

For Cedar:
Compute the square footage to be covered.
Add 10%-20% for waste.

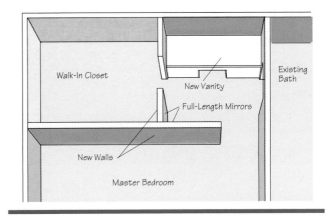

Measure and snap new lines on the ceiling perpendicular to the first lines at 72" and 75¹/₂" from the bathroom wall. These lines represent the dividing wall between the dressing and closet areas. Hold a plumb bob at one end of the line for the new front wall and mark the plumbed location on the floor. Repeat for the other line, then for the other end of each line. Snap lines on the floor at the marks. Use the plumb bob to locate the dividing wall on the floor in the same manner.

Use the lines on the ceiling and floor as guides to snap chalk lines on the side wall (opposite the bath wall) and back wall to mark the locations where the closet will connect to the existing walls (see illustration next page). The lines on the existing walls should be 1/2" outside the lines on the ceiling and floor. The additional space is needed to get a T into the existing wall (see inset). Remove the wall finish material between the lines as detailed on page 118.

2 Install a T in Existing Walls

A T is an assembly of studs and blocking used to firmly tie an intersecting wall into a straight wall. Build and install a T at the chalk lines snapped on the side and back existing walls as detailed on page 114.

1 Locate New Walls

Measure 72", then 75¹/₂" (based on a standard walk-in closet width of 6') out from the wall that will become the new closet/dressing room and mark the measurements on the ceiling. This should be done at each end of the wall. Snap chalk lines between the marks. These lines represent the wall between the closet/dressing room and the bedroom, and for the purposes of these instructions will be called the new front wall. The space that is closest to the bathroom will be the dressing area and the opposite side will be the walk-in closet. At the end closest to the bath, the lines should stop 30" from the existing wall. This area will remain open.

3 Cut & Mark Bottom Plates

At floor level, measure the distance from the existing side wall to the end of the new front wall. Keep the tape measure between the chalk lines on the floor. Mark the measured length on a 2x4. This will be the bottom plate for the front wall. If you are securing it to a concrete slab or other masonry material, the 2x4 should be pressure treated. Using a combination square, draw a perpendicular line through the mark and cut it with a circular saw.

The dividing wall will actually be two 24"-long walls with a 24" open space between them. Cut two more bottom plates to 24" long for the dividing wall.

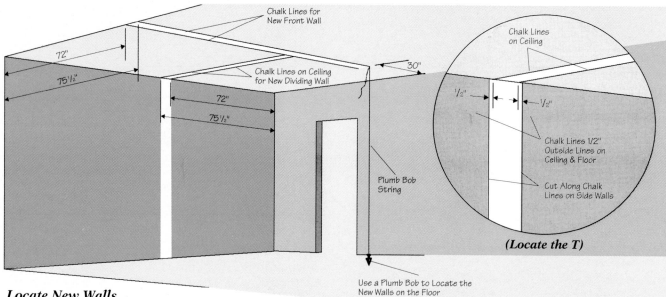

Locate New Walls

Chalk Lines for New Front Wall

72"

75 1/2"

Chalk Lines on Ceiling for New Dividing Wall

72"

75 1/2"

30"

Plumb Bob String

Use a Plumb Bob to Locate the New Walls on the Floor

Chalk Lines on Ceiling

1/2"   1/2"

Chalk Lines 1/2" Outside Lines on Ceiling & Floor

Cut Along Chalk Lines on Side Walls

(Locate the T)

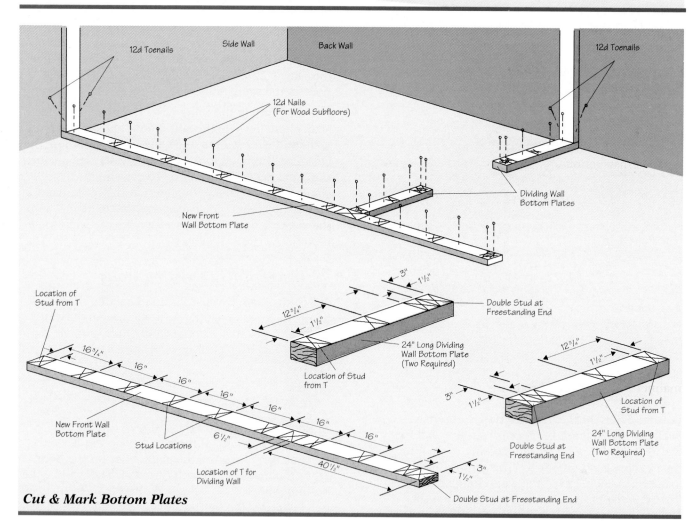

12d Toenails

Side Wall

Back Wall

12d Toenails

12d Nails (For Wood Subfloors)

Dividing Wall Bottom Plates

New Front Wall Bottom Plate

Location of Stud from T

16 3/4"

16"   16"   16"   16"   16"

New Front Wall Bottom Plate

Stud Locations

6 1/2"

Location of T for Dividing Wall

40 1/2"

12 3/4"   3"   1 1/2"

1 1/2"

Double Stud at Freestanding End

24" Long Dividing Wall Bottom Plate (Two Required)

Location of Stud from T

12 3/4"

1 1/2"

3"   1 1/2"

Double Stud at Freestanding End

24" Long Dividing Wall Bottom Plate (Two Required)

Location of Stud from T

3"

1 1/2"

Double Stud at Freestanding End

Cut & Mark Bottom Plates

At floor level, measure the length of the closet front wall and cut the bottom plate to fit. (Since few houses are perfectly square, you cannot use the length of the back wall.) Keep the tape measure between the chalk lines on the floor. Repeat the process for the dividing wall bottom plate. Measure from the back wall to the inside edge of the new front wall. Mark the stud locations on the bottom plates for the front wall and dividing walls.

4 Cut & Mark Top Plates

At ceiling level, measure the length of the front wall. Keep the tape measure between the chalk lines. Cut a 2x4 top plate to this length. Cut two pieces of 2x4 to 24" long. These will be the top plates for the two sections of the dividing wall.

Lay the front wall top plate side-by-side with the front wall bottom plate. If there is a variation in the length, center the plates with each other. (The end studs, however, will still be measured and marked at 1½" from the ends of the top plate.) Project the lines from the bottom plate onto the top plate. Write an X at each line as was done on the bottom plate. Repeat for the dividing wall top plates.

5 Install Plates

To install the plates, refer to the drawings on this and the previous page and then turn to page 113 for detailed instructions.

6 Install a T in New Walls

An additional T is required where the dividing wall intersects the new front wall. Measure the distance from the top surface of the bottom plate to the bottom surface of the top plate at the intersection. Cut the studs for the T to this dimension. Studs should be cut to the precise length, so measure carefully. Build the T in the same manner as before. Set into place and toenail into the top and bottom plates with 12d nails, two each end of each stud.

7 Install Studs

For a detailed explanation see page 84, Step 8.

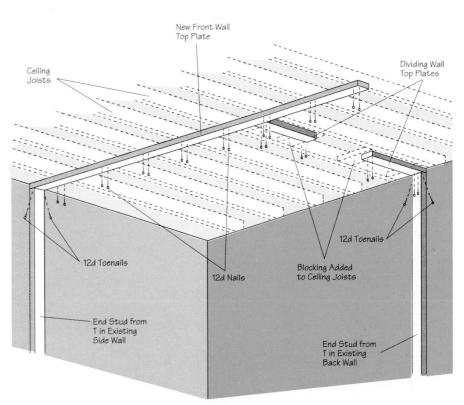

Ceiling Joists
New Front Wall Top Plate
Dividing Wall Top Plates
12d Toenails
12d Toenails
12d Nails
Blocking Added to Ceiling Joists
End Stud from T in Existing Side Wall
End Stud from T in Existing Back Wall

Cut & Mark Top Plates

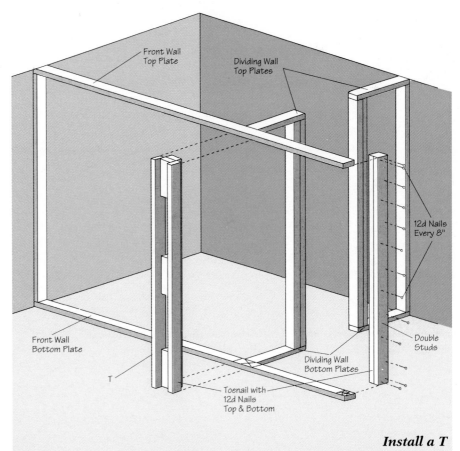

Front Wall Top Plate
Dividing Wall Top Plates
12d Nails Every 8"
Front Wall Bottom Plate
T
Double Studs
Dividing Wall Bottom Plates
Toenail with 12d Nails Top & Bottom

Install a T

8 *Install Finish Materials*

Install the finish wall materials of your choice on the inside and outside walls of the closet (see pages 121-124 for detailed instruction).

9 *Install Vanity*

The make-up vanity does not require plumbing and can be purchased, made to order, or built yourself, whichever you prefer. Set the vanity in place against the wall. Check the level. Place shims at the bottom as necessary to get the vanity level. Secure to the wall studs with six #10x3½" wood screws. The screws should go through the back brace of the vanity and into the wall studs behind the finish material. Use two screws at each stud.

You can install the vanity top in several ways depending on the type of cabinet and top you are using. For prefabricated tops follow the manufacturer's directions. Generally, there will be a piece of wood—a triangle or a strip—in each corner of the vanity. Wood screws go up through this piece of wood and into the vanity top from the bottom. The length of screw needed will depend on the thickness of this piece of wood and the thickness of the top. Be absolutely sure the screws are long enough to secure the top, but short enough so they will not come through the upper surface. Do not guess—measure twice. After the top has been installed, apply a bead of tub or tile sealant between the vanity top and the wall if desired.

10 *Install Mirrors*

The vanity mirror and full-length mirrors on the walls behind the vanity are a great aid for putting on make-up and getting dressed. We recommend that you have the mirrors installed by experts. The additional cost of installation should be minimal.

11 *Add Doors & Finish Closet*

Install closet doors, closet organizers, baseboard and other trim. Finally, install the carpet, if any. For details see pages 121-126.

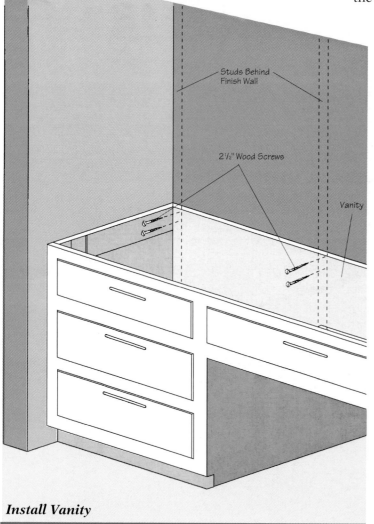

Studs Behind
Finish Wall

2½" Wood Screws

Vanity

Install Vanity

Freestanding Closet

With an emphasis on organization, utility, and mobility, the freestanding closet or wardrobe is making a comeback. You can custom design your wardrobe to match your particular decor.

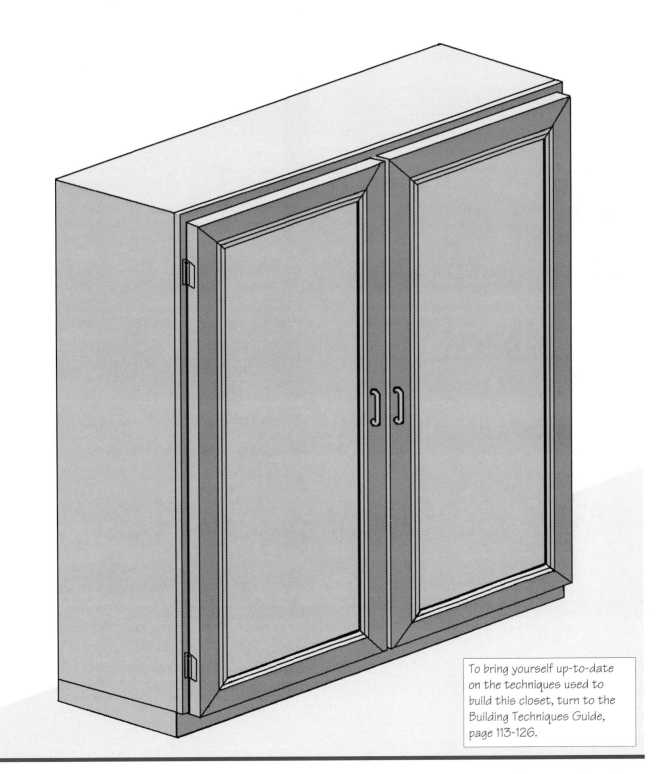

To bring yourself up-to-date on the techniques used to build this closet, turn to the Building Techniques Guide, page 113-126.

* Time required does not include drying time for glue.
* This project requires two workers.

Tools & Materials

- ☐ Hammer
- ☐ Combination Square
- ☐ Pencil
- ☐ Miter Saw
- ☐ Drill with Screwdriver Bit
- ☐ Nail Set
- ☐ 6d Finishing Nails
- ☐ (4) Casters (Optional)
- ☐ (3) 1x4x8 - Clear Grade
- ☐ (1) 1x4x8
- ☐ Clips (4 per shelf)
- ☐ (3) Sheets 3/4" A-A Plywood
- ☐ (3) Pairs Rod Brackets
- ☐ (12) Angle Brackets or Dowels or Clip Supports
- ☐ Wood Putty (If the closet will be painted)
- ☐ Putty Stick (For a stained or varnished closet)

- ☐ Measuring Tape
- ☐ Framing Square
- ☐ Level
- ☐ Table Saw
- ☐ Router
- ☐ 4d Finishing Nails
- ☐ Glue
- ☐ (24) #8x1¼" Wood Screws
- ☐ (4) 1x2x8
- ☐ 28' Metal Tracks for Shelves
- ☐ 8' Wood Round
- ☐ (2) Sheets 1/4" A-C Plywood
- ☐ Finish Materials

Doors:

- ☐ (4) 1x2x8
- ☐ (2) Sheets 1/4" A-A Plywood
- ☐ 2d Finishing Nails
- ☐ Door Handles

- ☐ (6) 2x4x8
- ☐ (35') 3/4" Cap Molding
- ☐ Hinges
- ☐ Clear Grade Softwood

NOTES: *For a fine furniture appearance, use hardwood-veneer plywood and substitute hardwood for clear grade lumber for the stiles and door frames. (In that case, you will need to drill holes in the stiles before nailing them into place.)*

All cuts, unless specifically stated otherwise, should be done on a table or radial arm saw. You will not be able to get the quality desired for this project by using a portable circular saw.

1 *Build Base*

Cut one piece of 1x4 to 64" long, another to 62½" long, and two more to 18¼" long. Apply glue to the mating surfaces and square with a framing square as you put the pieces together. Nail with 6d finishing nails. Cut two pieces of 1x2 to 62½" long and two more to 16" long. Use No. 8x1¼" wood screws every 8" to attach the 1x2 strips to the inside top of the base. Alternate the screws from the top of the 1x2 to the bottom. Attach the long strips first, then the short side strips.

Using a miter saw, cut four corner braces from 1x4. The cuts must be 45-degrees (see Install Casters, illustration next page). Set into place under the 1x2 strips and nail with 6d nails. Cut a piece of 3/4" plywood to 22"x71" long. Place on top of the base. The plywood should underhang 1/4" in the back, overhang 3¼" in front, and overhang 3½" on each side. Nail with 6d finishing nails every 8" on all four sides.

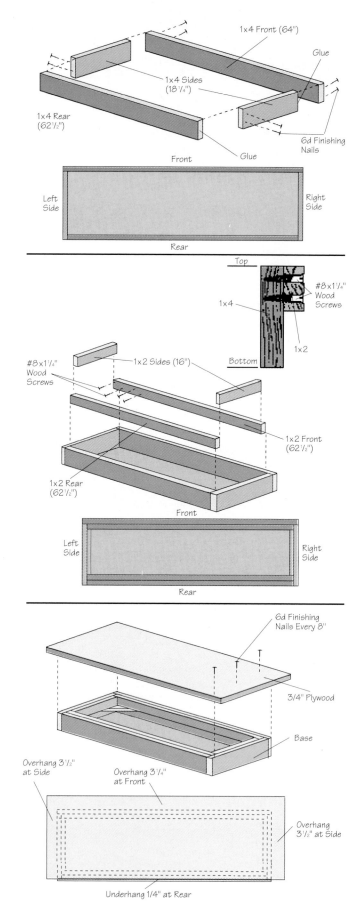

Build Base

2 Install Casters (Optional)

CAUTION: *The finished freestanding closet will be a heavy unit, particularly when filled with stored items. If you choose to add casters, select casters that will support the weight of a fully loaded closet.*

If the casters insert into a predrilled hole, drill a hole in each of the 1x4 corner braces and insert the casters per the manufacturer's directions. If they are attached by screws, use the screws provided.

3 Install Vertical Supports

Cut two strips of 3/4" plywood to 85½"x22¼", and another to 71"x22". The longer pieces are the side vertical supports and the third piece is the top. Using a router, cut a 1/4"-wide x 1/2"-deep rabbet along the back edge of the two longer pieces. (You can also cut the rabbets with two passes on a table saw.) Cut 3/4"-wide x 1/4"-deep rabbets along the inside edge of the top and bottom on each vertical support. The side vertical supports should be mirror opposites of each other.

Lay the base on its back on a flat surface. Apply glue to the rabbet in the bottom of each vertical support. Set the two vertical supports in place with the plywood bottom (on the base) snugly in the rabbet at the bottom of the vertical supports. Secure with 4d finishing nails. Apply glue to the rabbets at the

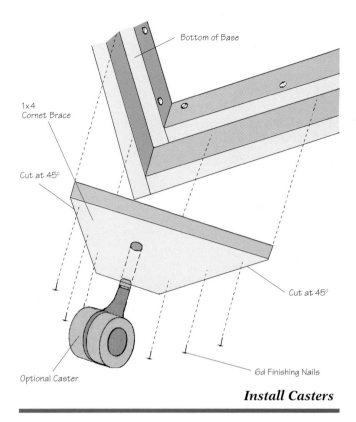

Install Casters

top of the vertical supports. Slide a piece of material that is 1/4" thick under the top and set the top into place in the rabbets. Square the unit with a framing square, then secure with 4d finishing nails.

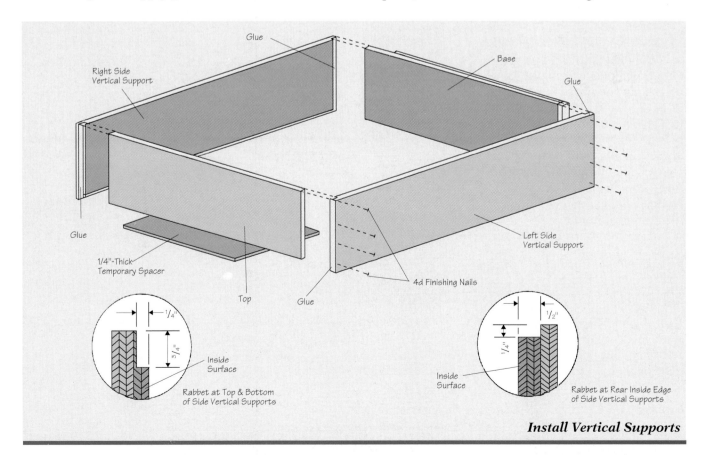

Install Vertical Supports

4 *Install Interior Dividers*

The interior dividers are made of 3/4" plywood and support the shelves and rods for the closet. Cut two pieces of 3/4" plywood to 84"x16". It will be easier to drill or route the dividers for shelving before installation. The shelves can be supported by angle brackets, clip supports, dowels, or metal tracks with clips. Angle brackets do not allow for easy adjustment of shelf heights. Dowels and clip supports can be adjustable, but require drilling numerous holes. Metal tracks are recommended because of the ease of installation and use.

Measure 4" from each edge and cut a dado of the correct width and depth for the metal tracks you have purchased. The dados should run the full length of the interior dividers. Screw the tracks into place with the screws provided by the manufacturer. Repeat for the second interior divider. Make sure that the bottom slot in all four tracks is at the exact same height so the shelves will lie level.

Measure 27", then 27³/₄" from each side (on the inside) and use a combination square to draw lines on the plywood base (see illustration). Repeat on the inside of the top. Apply glue to the top and bottom of the interior dividers and set in place on the lines. Use 1/4"-thick material as spacers under the dividers. They should be flush against the back and the metal tracks should be facing each other. Nail from the bottom and top with 4d finishing nails (four each end). Clean any excess glue.

Cut two strips of 1x2 and temporarily nail across the front in an X pattern, making sure the unit stays square as you nail. With help, lift the unit into an upright position.

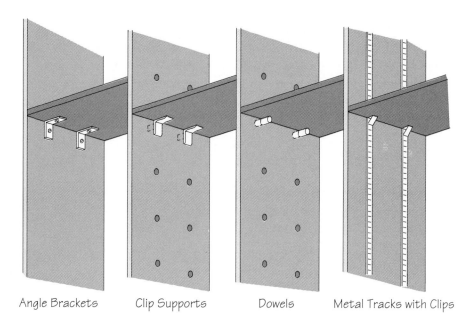

Angle Brackets   Clip Supports   Dowels   Metal Tracks with Clips

Shelf Installation Options

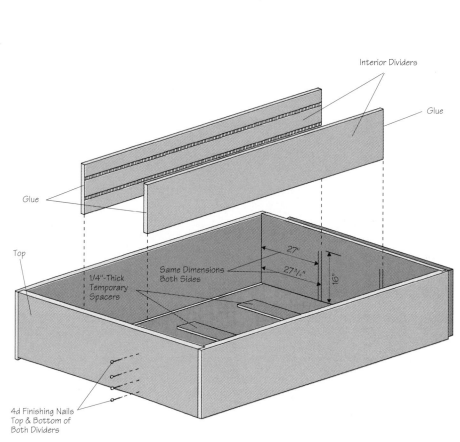

Interior Dividers

Glue

Glue

Glue

Top

1/4"-Thick Temporary Spacers

Same Dimensions Both Sides

27"

27³/₄"

16"

4d Finishing Nails Top & Bottom of Both Dividers

Install Interior Dividers

5 Install Shelves & Rods

Install angle brackets (or dowels or clip supports) at the locations shown on the right and left sides of the closet. Cut three shelves from 3/4" plywood to 16"x27". Attach two of the shelves to the angle brackets on the right side of the closet and the third to the angle brackets on the left side. Cut four to eight shelves (as desired) to 16"x15". Install clips into the metal tracks in the center section of the closet and set the shelves in place in the desired locations.

Cut three rods from wood round to 27" long. Slide two rod brackets on a rod, then secure to the closet in the locations shown (illustration next page) using the screws provided with the brackets (the screws must NOT be any longer than 3/4"). Repeat for the other two rods.

6 Install Plywood Backing

Cut one piece of 1/4" A-C plywood to 85$\frac{1}{2}$"x 43$\frac{5}{8}$" and another to 85$\frac{1}{2}$"x 27$\frac{7}{8}$". Apply glue to the back edge of the top, the rabbets in the back edges of the vertical supports, the back edges of the interior dividers, and in the 1/4" underlap at the rear of the base. Set the plywood on the back of the unit (see illustration following page). The finished (A) side of the plywood goes to the inside. It does not matter which side gets the wider or narrower strip. Nail the backing into the base, top, interior dividers, and side vertical supports with 2d finishing nails every 12". At the seam where the two pieces of backing meet, angle the nails slightly to make sure they "bite" into the interior divider.

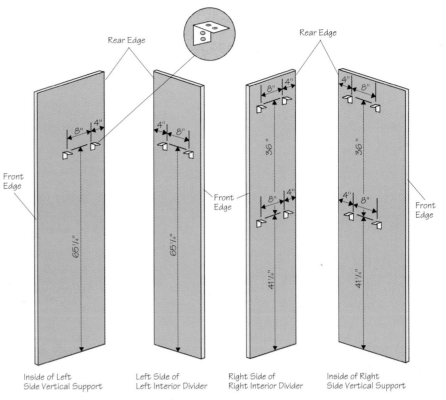

Install Shelf Brackets

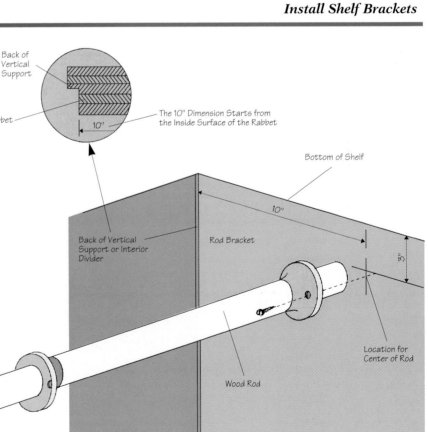

Install Hanging Rods

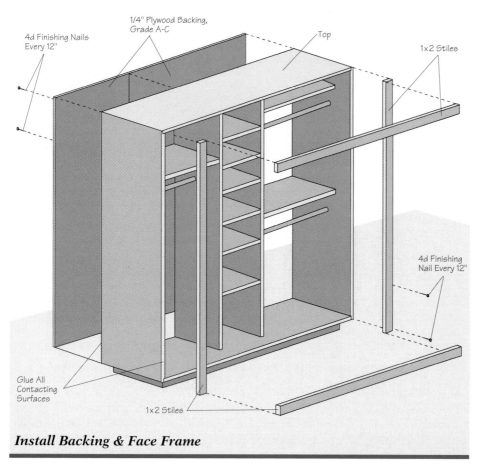

Install Backing & Face Frame

Labels on image:
- 4d Finishing Nails Every 12"
- 1/4" Plywood Backing, Grade A-C
- Top
- 1x2 Stiles
- 4d Finishing Nail Every 12"
- Glue All Contacting Surfaces
- 1x2 Stiles

7 Install Face Frame

Cut two pieces of clear-grade 1x2 to 85$^1/_2$". These are the stiles. Apply glue to the front edge of the side vertical supports. Set the stiles in place. The outside edge and the ends should be flush. Nail with 4d finishing nails every 12". Clean any excess glue. Cut two more pieces of 1x2 to 69" long each. These are the top and bottom rails. Install between the stiles in the same manner. Apply 3/4"-wide screen molding to the interior dividers and shelves as detailed on page 103.

8 Build & Install Doors

Using a miter saw, cut two pieces of clear grade 2x4 to 84$^1/_2$" long. Cut two more pieces to 35$^1/_2$". Using a router, cut a 1/4" wide by 3/8" deep groove along the inside edge of all four pieces. Cut a 1/4" A-A plywood panel to 78$^1/_4$"x 29$^1/_4$". Apply glue to the grooves and assemble as shown. Use 2d finishing nails in the corners. Nail from the top and bottom only. Repeat the process for the second door.

Once the glue has dried, cut a 3/8"-deep by 3/4"-wide rabbet along the top, bottom, and one side on the inside of each door. The rabbet will allow the doors to recess into the cabinet by 3/8" when closed. This

completes the standard doors. They can be finished in a virtually unlimited number of ways by using molding and/or routing the edges of the 2x4s. Finish the unit to suit your taste.

A variety of hinges and door knob and door pulls are available at hardware and home center stores. Hinges can be visible or hidden. Select the style of hardware that best suits your needs, then install per the manufacturer's directions.

9 Finish Closet

Using the appropriately sized nail set, recess all visible nail heads. If you are going to paint the cabinet, fill the holes with wood putty first, then apply a primer and two coats of your selected finish. For stain or varnish, apply the finish BEFORE filling the holes where the nails were set. After the finish is complete, fill the holes with a precolored putty stick to match the finish. Then, add extras, such as hooks or a belt rack to the door, depending upon your needs.

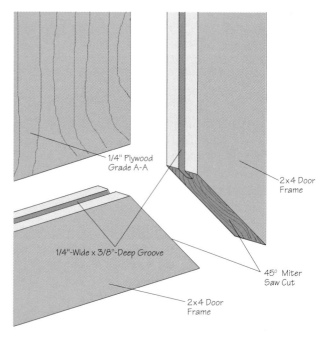

Labels on image:
- 1/4" Plywood Grade A-A
- 2x4 Door Frame
- 1/4"-Wide x 3/8"-Deep Groove
- 45° Miter Saw Cut
- 2x4 Door Frame

Build Doors

Organizer Installation Guide

Three types of closet organizers—hand-built, laminate and coated-wire—are featured in this book. Depending upon the type of material you have chosen to use, there are different ways to install each system. The techniques included here follow the logical order you will take to install a closet organizer from start to finish. As you proceed in a project, certain steps will refer you to this part of the book. Many of the techniques described are common knowledge. If not, read further for detailed instructions. Then, return to the original project.

Hand-Built Wood Systems

Tips for Working with Hand-Built Systems

1. Longer shelves, particularly a shelf that goes on top of a vertical divider, should be set in place first, but not nailed. It could be impossible to get the shelf into the closet after a vertical divider is secured.

2. Nail shelves starting with the lowest shelf and moving upward. This allows lifting a higher shelf out of the way so you can swing a hammer.

3. If possible, use a table saw so that the plywood cuts are more accurate.

4. Stain or paint the components before installing, then touch up afterward.

5. Tap pilot holes for wood screws, then install screws using a power screwdriver or a variable speed drill with screwdriver bit.

Select & Cut Plywood

There are many types of plywood finishes available in a range of qualities. The most common finish for 3/4"-thick plywood is A-C fir or pine. This means that one side, the A side, is a high-quality finish with knot holes that are plugged or patched. The other side, the C side, is only average quality and will have some knot holes. Cut and install the A-C plywood so that the best side is in view. You can buy plywood surfaced with birch, oak and other hardwoods. These can be found with quality finishes on one or both sides, but are usually more costly. If you are building an open closet or want your closet to be a showplace, the extra investment may be worthwhile.

To cut plywood, use a table saw equipped with a fine-tooth plywood blade. If you do not have a table saw, have the lumber supplier cut the plywood for you. Most suppliers will provide this service free or at a minimum cost. Those who can do neither may use a circular saw. Before cutting, clamp a 2x4 to the plywood as a guide for the saw. Take your time, the cuts must be accurate.

Cut & Install Rod & Shelf Supports

This technique provides solid structural support for both rod and shelf, while being reasonably easy to install. For rod and shelf supports that will attach to the wall, measure the depth of the closet. Cut a 1x4 to the measured distance. Use lumber that does not have knots in it. For rod and shelf supports that will attach to a shelf tower or other type of vertical divider, cut the 1x4 to the depth of the shelf tower.

Use the following chart to determine distance from the back of the support to the centerline of the rod:

Closet Depth	Dimension
23" or More	12"
20" to 23"	1/2 Closet Depth
20" or Less	10"

Measure the correct distance from the back of the rod and shelf support. Draw a perpendicular line through the mark using a combination square. Measure 1½" up from the bottom of the 1x4 and draw another line through the first line. Drill a hole through the marks, with the center of the hole at the point where the two lines intersect. The diameter of the hole should be slightly larger than the diameter of the rod you are using. For wood use 1½" diameter rods.

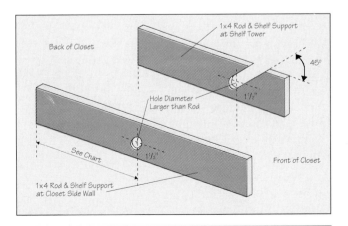

For each pair of rod and shelf supports, one must be cut to allow the rod to slip through. Draw 45-degree tangents to each side of the hole. The lines should slope toward the front of the support. Use a circular saw to cut along each line. Be sure the support is firmly clamped prior to sawing to avoid a slip. When installed, one end of the rod will be placed in the support with the drilled hole only. The other end will slide into the support with the cutout.

For closet side walls, set the rod and shelf support in place against a level line marking the location of the bottom of the shelf. Nail with two 10d finishing nails at each stud. Use a stud finder to locate the wall studs. At the ends, move the nails back from the edge of the support and angle as necessary so that you hit the stud. At shelf towers or other wood vertical supports, drill pilot holes in the rod and shelf support at the screw locations. Place a wood screw into each pilot hole. Set the support in place against a level line and drive the wood screws using a power screwdriver or a variable-speed drill with a screwdriver bit.

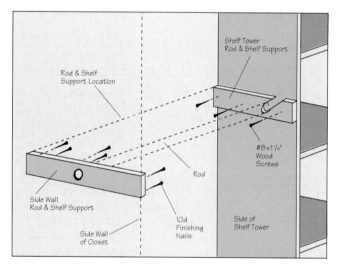

Install Rod & Shelf

Measure the distance between the rod and shelf supports, including the thicknesses of the supports. Cut a rod to the measured length ($1\frac{1}{2}$" wood round is suggested, though you can use a different size). Other types of rods, such as galvanized pipe, can also be used. The only criteria is that the material is strong enough to hold the weight of your clothing. Set one end of the rod into the rod and shelf support which has only a drilled hole. The other end of the rod should slide down through the cutout in the opposite support and rests in the bottom of the originally drilled hole.

Measure the length necessary for the shelf (from wall to wall, wall to vertical support, or vertical support to vertical support) at the front and back. There may be a slight variance between the front and back since walls often are not perfectly square. If the length is more than 4', an additional 1x4 is needed at the rear wall. Cut the 1x4 to the necessary length; nail with two 10d finishing nails at each stud.

The maximum length that the rod and shelf can extend without an additional vertical support is 8'. (Most wood rods, however, cannot support 8' of clothing without additional support.) Cut a piece of 16"-wide plywood to the required shelf length. Set in place on top of the rod and shelf supports. Nail down through the shelf and into the supports with 4d finishing nails. Use four for each end. Do not nail into the cutouts that were made for the rods. If there is a 1x4 at the back wall, drive a 4d finishing nail through the shelf and into the 1x4 at 12" intervals.

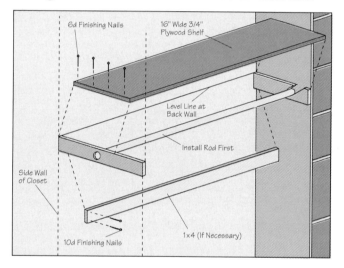

Cut Shelves

Measure and cut shelves to fit using 16"-wide plywood. Set the shelves in place to test for fit, but do not nail yet. Once all the shelves are cut and in place, start with the lowest shelf and secure with four 4d finishing nails at each end of each shelf. For shelves that span more than 4', install a 1x4 on the wall at the back of the shelf using 10d finishing nails, then drive 4d finishing nails through the shelf and into the 1x4 every 12". Work one shelf at a time, starting with the lowest shelf, so that upper shelves can be lifted out of the way when nailing. Install the side wall shelves first. Finally, install the upper shelf at the back wall. Toenail this shelf into the upper shelves on the side walls with 4d finishing nails.

Attach Trim Strips to Plywood

Measure one of the plywood vertical supports and cut a strip of 3/4"-wide screen (cap) molding to that length. Apply carpenter's glue to the back of the molding and set in place. Secure with a few 2d finishing nails to hold the molding in place while the glue dries. Repeat until each exposed plywood edge is covered.

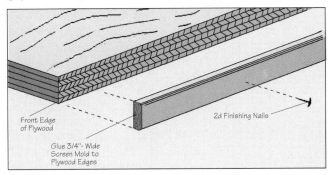

Front Edge
of Plywood

2d Finishing Nails

Glue 3/4"- Wide
Screen Mold to
Plywood Edges

Install Shelves

Storage shelves can be installed in a variety of ways. The following methods are some of the most common.

Metal Tracks: The best way to install multiple shelves is to use metal tracks. Tracks allow you to install a variable number of shelves which can be adjusted to virtually any desired height. The tracks are installed by routing dados of the correct width and depth into the wood dividers that are on each side of the shelves. For 16"-deep shelves, the dados should be 4" from the front and back. Set the metal tracks into the dados and secure with wood screws. (The size of the wood screws depends on the size of the metal track.) Shelves are supported by clips that snap into the tracks.

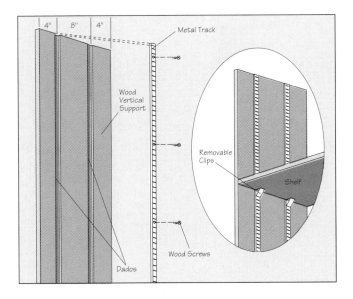

4"   8"   4"

Metal Track

Wood
Vertical
Support

Removable
Clips

Shelf

Wood Screws

Dados

Dowels: The use of wood dowels also allows for adjustment of shelf height, but to a lesser degree. First, draw vertical lines on the vertical supports at 4" from the front and 4" from the rear. For fixed shelves, mark the desired locations on the vertical lines. For adjustable shelves, mark the vertical lines every 2", or by the amount of adjustment desired. Drill a 1/2"-deep hole at each mark. The center of the hole should be every point where two lines cross. The size of the drill bit should be the same as the diameter of the dowels you are using. You will need four dowels for each shelf. Cut the required number of dowels to 1" long. Insert into the proper holes in the vertical supports. Cut the shelf to length and set on top of the dowels.

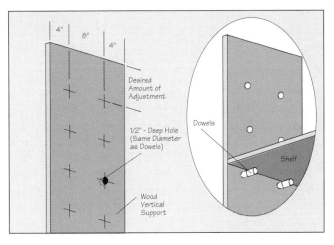

4"   8"   4"

Desired
Amount of
Adjustment

1/2" - Deep Hole
(Same Diameter
as Dowels)

Wood
Vertical
Support

Dowels

Shelf

Clip Supports: Clip supports are installed in the same manner as the dowels. Each support has a round extension that is designed to go into a hole in the vertical support. Drill holes as described for dowels, then insert the clip supports at the desired locations. Cut the shelf to length and set into place on top of the clip supports.

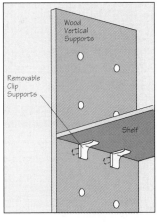

Wood
Vertical
Supports

Removable
Clip
Supports

Shelf

Dados: Although the use of dados to install shelving does not allow for height adjustment, it is the sturdiest way to install a shelf. Dados are perfect for constructing shelf towers. First, mark the desired shelf locations on the vertical dividers on each side. Measure down the thickness of the shelf material (3/4" plywood is suggested) and make another mark. Use a framing square to draw a perpendicular line through each mark. Use a router or table saw equipped with a dado-cutting blade to cut 1/4"-deep dados at each pair of lines. If using a router, clamp a guide board in place before cutting. Place a line of glue inside the dado and along the edge of the shelf. Insert the shelf into the dado, tapping lightly with a hammer if necessary. Secure each side of each shelf with three 4d finishing nails to hold the shelf firmly in place while the glue dries.

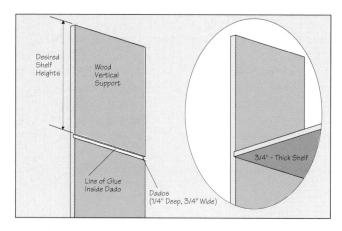

Furring Strips: Like dados, furring strips are not adjustable. They can be made from 1x1 or 1x2 stock, or 45-degree molding. Two furring strips are required for each shelf. Cut the required number of furring strips to 12" long. Install each strip against the vertical support, at the level of the bottom of the shelf. The strips align with the rear of the shelf and underhang 4" in the front of the shelf. Tap pilot holes with 4d nails, then secure with 1¼" wood screws, three each furring strip. Set the shelf in place on top of the furring strips. Nail through the shelf and into the furring strips with 4d finishing nails, four each end. If you prefer, you also can nail through the sides of the vertical supports and into the edges of the shelves.

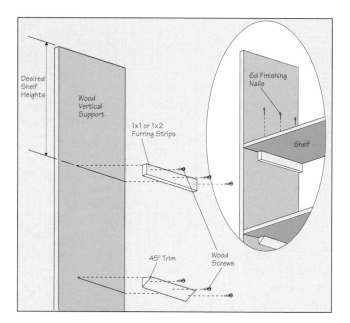

Angle Brackets: While angle brackets do not provide for adjustment, they are strong and relatively easy to install. Mark the bottom of the shelves on the vertical supports. Set the angle brackets in place one at a time, one 4" from the rear and one 4" from the front, and mark the mounting hole locations on the vertical supports. Remove the angle brackets and tap pilot holes with 4d nails. Set the angle brackets back into place and secure with the screws provided or purchase 3/4"-long wood screws of the appropriate diameter. A variable speed drill with a screwdriver bit will make the job much easier. Cut the shelf to fit and set on top of the angle brackets. Use a pencil to mark the bracket mounting hole on the bottom of the shelf. Remove the shelf and tap pilot holes with 4d nails. Set the shelf back into place and secure with wood screws.

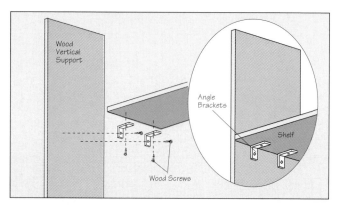

General: The methods above are designed for shelves that will attach to a wood surface on each side, such as a shelf tower. If attaching to a drywall surface, use 1x2 wood furring strips nailed into studs with 10d finishing nails. If there are no studs where needed, use wall anchors or toggle bolts.

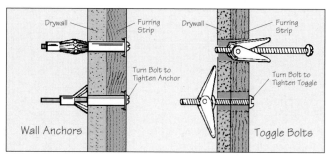

For masonry surfaces, set the 1x2 in place and drill three 1/8" holes through it, marking the masonry surface beyond with the bit as you drill through the opposite side of the wood. Remove the 1x2 and drill a hole at each of the three marks with a 1/4" masonry bit. Insert a plastic anchor into each hole. Set the 1x2 back into place and secure to the plastic anchors with wood screws.

Install a Hand-Built Shelf Tower

Hand-built shelf towers are secured to the back closet wall using furring strips. The furring strips are secured to the top and bottom of the wall with plastic anchors and screws. They may be attached to the shelf tower in different ways. One method involves notching the vertical dividers, then installing the furring strips into the notches with wood screws. The notches should be cut before the shelf tower is assembled.

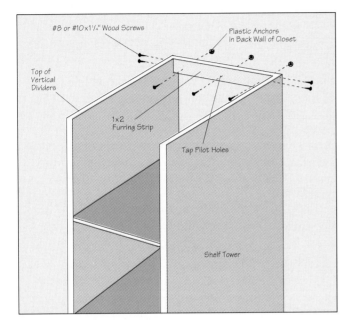

An easier method, though not quite as sturdy, is to cut the furring strips to fit from inside surface to inside surface of the shelf tower. Install the furring strips using two wood screws through the side of the tower at each end. Set the shelf tower in place and drill three pilot holes through each of the furring strips with a 1/8" bit. Remove the shelf tower and drill the holes in the wall with a 1/4" bit, then insert a plastic anchor into each hole. Set the tower back into place and secure to the plastic anchors with wood screws.

Build a Drawer

For a closed place in which to store objects, drawers can be built into the shelf tower. Two simple drawer assemblies are described here: one that requires rabbets and one that does not require rabbets. Both types result in a drawer that simply slides in and out on top of a shelf. Install the shelves first (they must be fixed rather than adjustable).

Those accomplished with woodwork may prefer to build a more elaborate drawer system than the ones indicated here.

Build a Drawer with Rabbets

Measure the width, height and depth of the shelf area where the drawer is to be located. Subtract 1/4" from the width and height to get the finished dimensions for the drawer. Cut two pieces of 3/4" plywood to the finished drawer depth less 1", and to the finished drawer height. Cut a 3/8"-wide by 1/4"-deep rabbet in the bottom of each piece. These are the drawer sides. Cut 1/2"-wide by 3/8"-deep rabbets on the inside front of each piece.

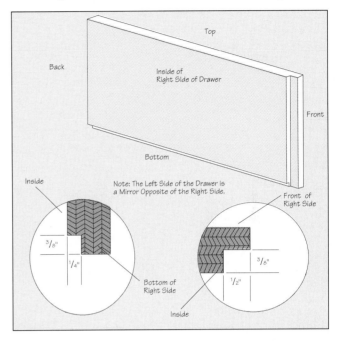

Cut two more pieces of 3/4" plywood to the finished drawer height and width. One piece is the drawer front and one is the drawer back. Cut 3/8"-wide by 1/4"-deep rabbets in the bottom of these two pieces. On the front piece, cut a 3/8"-wide by 1/2"-deep rabbet on each end at the inside surface. Use a jigsaw to cut a hand grip out of the top of the front piece. Sand the cut until it is smooth.

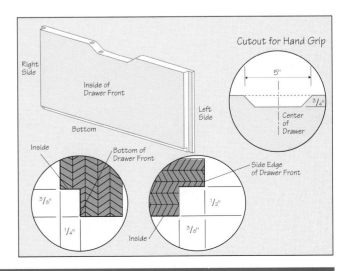

Place a bead of carpenter's glue along the back edges of the side pieces of the drawer. Nail the drawer back into the side pieces with 4d finishing nails. Place carpenter's glue in the rabbets in the front edges of the side pieces. Set the front piece in place and nail from the side with 4d finishing nails. Be sure the assembly remains square. Use a nail punch to countersink the nails in front. Fill the holes with wood putty if you plan to paint the drawers. If staining, use a matching color stick to fill holes after the drawers have been stained.

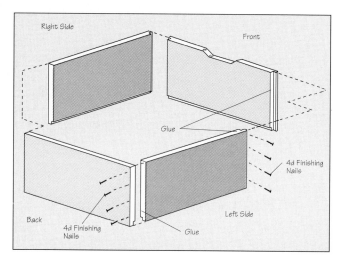

The drawer bottom will fit inside the rabbets at the bottom of the side, back and front pieces. Turn the unit upside down and measure for the bottom. Cut a piece of 1/4" plywood to the measured length and width. Place a bead of glue all around the bottom of the drawer in the rabbets. Set the bottom in place and nail with 2d finishing nails, angling the nails toward the outside slightly. Sand the bottom of the drawer and the top of the shelf until smooth.

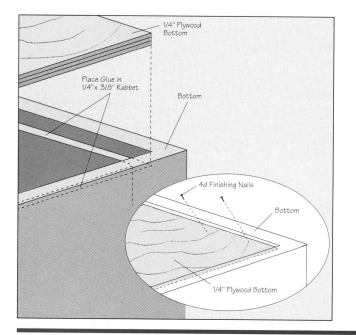

Build a Drawer without Rabbets

Building a drawer without rabbets is easier than making one with rabbets, but it will not stand up to heavy usage. Measure the width, height and depth of the shelf space where the drawer is to be located. Subtract 1/4" from the width and height to get the finished dimensions for the drawer. Cut two pieces of 3/4" plywood: to the finished drawer depth less 1½", and the finished drawer height. These will be the drawer sides. Cut two more pieces of 3/4" plywood to the height and width of the finished drawer. One piece is the drawer front and one is the drawer back. Use a jigsaw to cut a hand grip out of the top of the front piece. Sand the cut until smooth.

Place a bead of carpenter's glue along the back edges of the side pieces and nail the drawer back into the side pieces with 4d finishing nails. Place a bead of carpenter's glue along the front edges of the side pieces and nail together with 4d finishing nails. Make sure the assembly remains square. Use a nail punch to countersink the nails in front. Fill the holes with wood putty if you plan to paint the drawers. If staining, use a matching color stick to fill holes after the drawers have been stained.

Cut two strips of 1/4" plywood to 1/2" wide by the inside width of the drawer (or use small stock lumber or molding). Cut two more to 1/2" wide by the inside length of the drawer. Secure the strips along the inside bottom of all four sides of the drawer with 3/4" wood screws. Measure the width and length on the inside of the drawer. Cut a piece of 1/4" plywood to the measured dimensions. Place a bead of carpenter's glue on top of the strips previously nailed into place. With the drawer upright, lower the bottom onto the top of the strips and secure with 2d finishing nails. Sand the bottom of the drawer and top of the shelf until smooth.

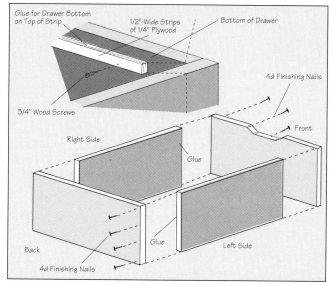

Install a Hand-Built Shoe Rack

Using an adjustable miter saw, cut each end of a 12"-long 1x2 to a 15-degree angle . If you do not have an adjustable miter saw, make the cut 1/4" from square on one edge. Repeat the process to cut a second furring strip.

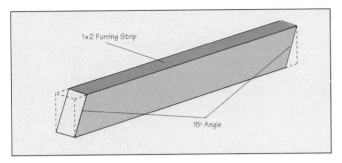

Tap three pilot holes into the side of each furring strip. Set the furring strips in place against the vertical supports at the desired location for the shoe rack. There should be a minimum clearance of 6" off the floor for cleaning purposes. Secure the strips with 1 ¼" wood screws in each pilot hole. At stud walls, use 10d finishing nails.

Measure the length needed for the shoe rack. Cut a strip of 16"-wide, 3/4" plywood to the measured distance. (1x12 shelving will work for smaller shoe sizes, but change the length of the 1x2 furring strips to 9".) Measure 6" in from the rear of the shelf at each end and place a mark. (Use 4" for 1x12 shelving.) Cut a strip of 1x1 or smaller stock to the length of the shelf. This will be used as a heel stop. Nail the heel stop onto the shelf at the marks using 2d finishing nails. Set the shelf in place on the furring strips and drive 4d finishing nails through the shelf and into the strips, four nails each end.

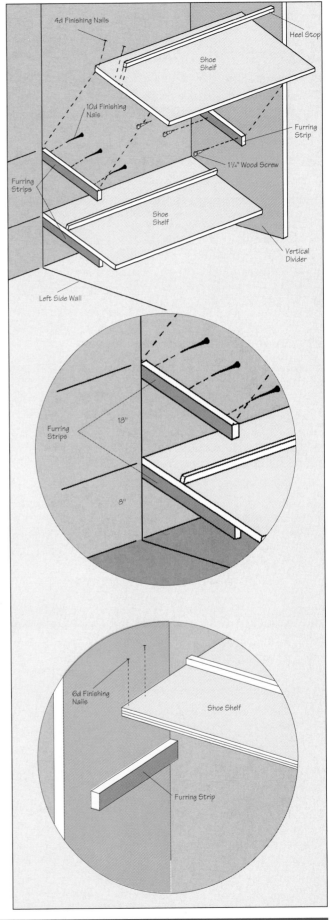

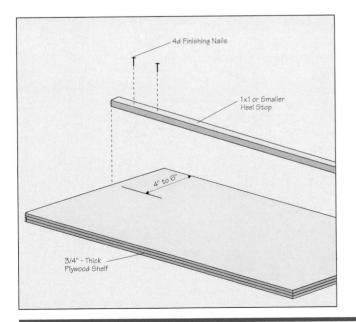

Laminated Systems

Tips for Working with Laminated Systems

1. Laminated systems are usually made with a plastic laminate surface material over particleboard. Because particleboard can chip more easily than solid wood, be very careful when making hardware connections such as installing a screw into the particleboard.

2. Particleboard is very heavy. You will probably need help lifting and installing completed laminated components.

3. Most laminated systems are fairly easy to install following the manufacturer's directions which may vary significantly from one manufacturer's design to another. Read them prior to starting any assembly or installation activity.

Secure a Laminated Shelf Tower

Laminated shelf towers come in a variety of widths. For wider closets, use a wider shelf tower; for narrow closets, use a more narrow shelf tower. Laminated units also vary in height. Depending upon the height you desire, you may have to stack two shelf towers vertically since many manufacturers do not offer single units that are tall.

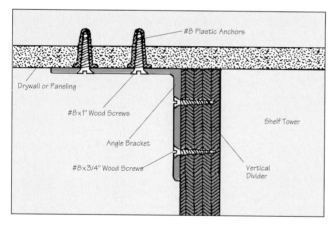

You may install shelves, drawers, swinging doors, and hooks into the shelf tower. Study the options and build the shelf tower to meet your needs.

Some systems do not provide for the option of securing a shelf tower to the closet back wall. Although the tower can be set into place and used as is, it is a good idea to secure the tower to the wall to avoid any possibility of tipping over. You will need the following additional materials: two angle brackets, four No. 8 plastic anchors, four No. 8 by 1" wood screws, and four No. 8 by 3/4" wood screws.

Measure and mark the desired location for the shelf tower in the closet. Use a level to draw a plumb, vertical line at the mark. Set the shelf tower in place in the closet against the vertical line. Hold an angle bracket in place on one side, near the top. Mark the hole locations on the shelf tower and the back closet wall. Repeat on the other side of the shelf tower. Remove the tower. Drill a 1/4" hole at each of the four marks on the closet back wall. Insert a plastic anchor into each hole. Set the shelf tower back into place. Secure an angle bracket to the anchors on one side of the tower with two 1" wood screws. Repeat on the other side. Finally, secure each angle bracket to the shelf tower with two 3/4" wood screws.

Install Rods

Adjustable hanging rods are used with laminated organizer systems. Common sizes include a small rod that adjusts from 18" to 30", one that adjusts from 30" to 48", and a large rod that adjusts from 48" to 72", though what you find may differ. Other types of rods for laminate systems are not adjustable, but are cut to fit.

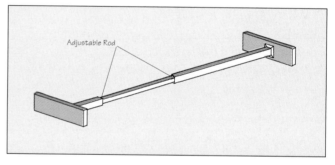

Assemble & Install Shoe Shelves

For most systems, shoe shelves consist of a shelf or two with side supports. They will vary depending on the manufacturer. Assemble and install them according to manufacturer's instructions.

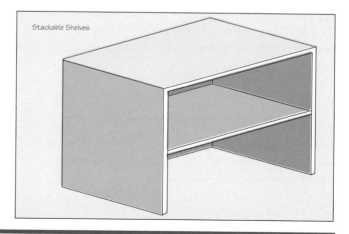

Coated-Wire Systems

NOTE: *Although most coated-wire organizer systems are based on the same general principles, manufacturer's installation instructions will vary slightly. Read instructions before beginning work.*

Tips for Working with Coated-Wire Systems

1. Use bolt cutters to cut shelves. A hacksaw may be used but it takes considerably longer. Many building supply dealers will cut the shelf materials to the length you specify at the time of purchase.

2. If you have more than a couple of shelves to install, use a variable speed drill with a screwdriver bit. A regular, hand screwdriver is too slow for all but the smallest jobs.

3. Mark back clip locations carefully. If your measurements are off, shelf installation may be difficult.

4. Do not insert the shelf into the clips prematurely; it is difficult to remove a shelf once it has been inserted into the clips.

5. When installing a shelf into the clips, start at one end and install one at a time, lightly popping the front edge of the shelf (opposite the clip) with your hand.

6. If you do not have a helper, find a prop to hold shelves up and out of the way when installing end brackets, support poles, etc.

Install a Coated-Wire Shelf

NOTE: *A storage shelf and an integral rod and shelf are installed in the same manner. The only variation is the orientation of joiner plates for support braces.*

Decide exactly where the shelf will be located. Measure the shelf height at one end and mark the measurement on the wall. Place a level at the marked height, then draw a line along the edge of the level. If you do not have a long level, use a straight board and place your level on top of the board. Continue to draw the line on the wall, across the full length of the shelf.

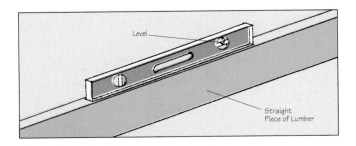

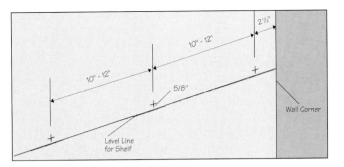

Install Clips: Start 2 1/2" from one end of the shelf if against a wall, and 1" if not. Place a mark just above the line. Place additional marks every 12" (every 10" if the length of the shelf is less than 4' long). Place a final mark at 2 1/2" from the opposite wall, or 1" if the end of the shelf is open. At each mark measure 5/8" above the line and make a cross. For drywall, paneling, particleboard, or a similar material over hollow walls, use a 1/4" wood bit to drill a hole at the center of each cross. For masonry walls use a 1/4" masonry bit. For solid wood walls, 1" thick or thicker, use a 5/32" wood bit.

For drywall, paneling, particleboard or a similar material, over hollow walls, place a back clip into each hole, tapping lightly with a hammer if necessary. There are two ways to install clips onto masonry walls: place a back clip into the drilled hole and secure with a screw, or place a plastic anchor in each hole and use a screw to secure a down clip to the plastic anchor. For solid, 1" thick or thicker, wood walls, use a wood screw to install a down clip into each hole. You can drive the screw with a screwdriver, but a variable-speed drill with a screwdriver bit will do the job faster and more easily. Hold a clip in place with one hand, to keep it from spinning around, and screw with the other. Plastic anchors, clips and screws are furnished with organizer kits, or can be bought in quantity if you are purchasing the organizer components separately.

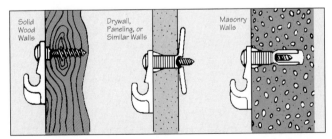

Measure the length for the shelf. Subtract 1 1/2" if the shelf will abut a wall at both ends. Subtract 3/4" if the shelf will abut a wall at one end. If the shelf will not abut a wall, use the given measurement as is. Using a pair of bolt cutters, cut the coated-wire shelf to the desired length. You can also cut the shelf with a hacksaw, but it takes longer.

Slide plastic end caps over the cut ends of the steel wire. This will cover the rough edges of the cuts. End caps are available in two sizes: large or small. Large end caps are needed at the rod portion of an integral rod and shelf.

Place the back of the shelf just above the clips in the wall. For longer shelves, two people may be required: one to hold the shelf in place and the other to anchor the shelf into the clips. Starting at one end, snap the back wire of the shelf into the clips by setting the shelf vertically on the groove in the clips and tapping the front of the shelf with your hand. It should snap into place without too much force. Work one clip at a time until you reach the other end.

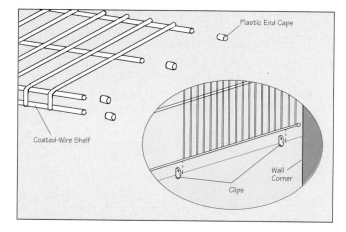

Install an End Bracket

For all shelf ends that abut a wall, an end bracket is needed to anchor the shelf. Lower the shelf and level the end at the wall. Slide the end bracket onto the shelf. Use a pencil to mark the mounting holes in the bracket onto the wall. Lift the shelf out of the way and drill a 1/4" hole at each mark. Insert a plastic anchor in each hole. Set the end bracket in place and secure with a screw in each mounting hole. Lower the shelf again and snap into the end bracket.

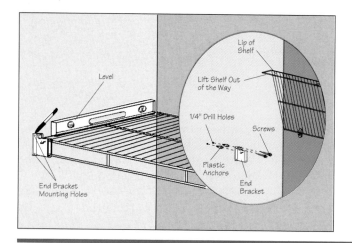

Install a Support Brace

A support brace is required every 3½' along a shelf and at shelf ends that do not abut a wall. Place the joiner plates on the lip of the shelf. For an integral rod and shelf, turn the plates vertically (left). For storage shelves, the plates are oriented horizontally (right). Insert a joiner plate bolt through the plates from the front. Place the smaller end of the support brace over the bolt at the rear. Thread a nut onto the bolt and hand tighten.

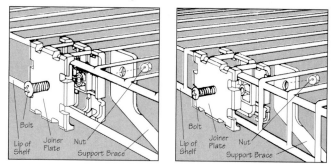

Place a down clip upside down on the rear wire of the shelf directly opposite the location of the support brace at the front. Lower the shelf and level it. On the wall, mark the location of the hole for the down clip, then mark the location of the lower hole

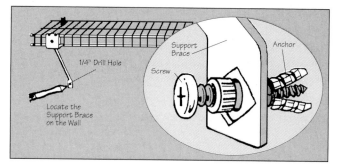

of the support brace. Lift the shelf and twist the support brace out of the way. Drill a 1/4" hole at each mark. Insert a plastic anchor in both holes. Lower the shelf and twist the support brace back into place. Attach the down clip and then the lower end of the support brace. Tighten the bolt and nut that holds the top end of the support brace onto the joiner plates. Some systems snap into place on the front of the shelf rather than using joiner plates.

Install a Corner Support Bracket

A corner support bracket is used to tie two shelves together in a corner. Install the shelves in the normal manner. One shelf will extend to the wall corner and the other shelf will abut the first. Install a corner support bracket at the corner where the two shelves meet. You will need to work the support bracket into place, lifting and separating the shelves slightly. The support bracket rests between the wires of the shelves and does not require any fasteners.

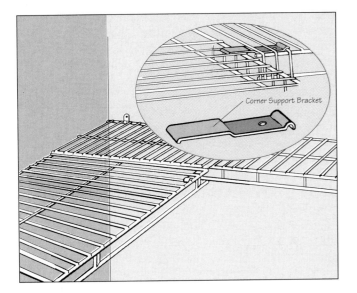

Install a Support Pole

A support pole should be used when installing a series of shelves. Support poles are generally stronger than the braces.

Slide the plastic end caps onto each end of the pole. Temporarily set the pole against the shelves. Level each shelf and mark it on the pole. Drill a pilot hole 5/8" above each mark. Set a down clip in place at each mark and secure with a screw. Set the pole back against the shelves and snap the front wire of each shelf into the down clips.

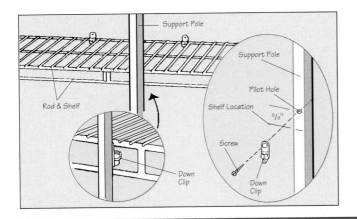

Install a Shoe Shelf

A coated-wire shoe shelf is simply a 12" storage shelf turned upside down. Set the shelf against the wall with the lip on the floor, facing away from the wall. Draw a line along the top of the shelf. Place a mark 2½" from ends that abut a wall and 1" from open ends, and every 10" between. Install a back clip at each location using the same directions as those described above for shelves.

Slide the shoe shelf support brace between the steel wires about 2" from the rear of the shelf and several inches from one end. The brace should be on the opposite face of the shelf from the lip. It goes in at an angle and is twisted to get the wires into the grooves on the sides of the brace. Slide the brace forward and snap into place on the larger steel wire running the length of the shelf in the middle. Install the second shoe shelf support brace an equal distance from the other end of the shelf. Finally, snap the shelf into place on the back clips that were installed in the wall, then lower so that the shoe shelf support braces touch the wall. For shoe shelves longer than 4' or 5', additional support braces may be necessary depending on the weight of the shoes to be placed on the shelf.

Two 18"-long shoe shelves will hold four pairs of shoes. Set the second shelf on top of the first with the lip down and facing away from the back wall. Again, draw a line along the top and mark three clip locations. Install the second shelf in the same manner as the first.

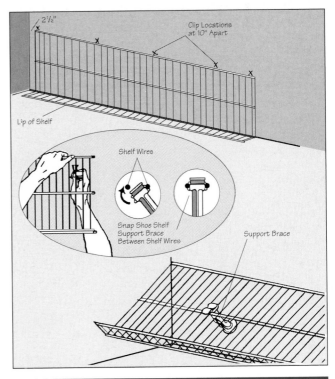

Build a Wire-Basket Drawer System

Wire-basket drawer systems normally come in 4-, 7-, and 10-runner systems. The numbers represent the maximum number of drawers that can be used. If you want deeper drawers, there will be fewer drawers than the number of runners. The components for these systems are usually packaged separately because they are modular systems. Purchase the folowing: a 4-, 7-, or 10-runner side frame set, a cross brace set in the width you desire; the appropriate number of single, double, or triple wire-basket drawers in a matching width; drawer stops; floor protector caps (if not using casters); caster bracket set (optional), and casters (optional).

The cross brace set includes four cross braces and four T and four L connectors for putting the cross braces and side frames together. Using a hammer, tap the bottom of a T into each end of two cross braces. Then, tap an L into each end of the other two cross braces. The cross braces with the L connectors go into the top of the side runners.

The top of the side frame is the edge with the runner closest to the end. Tap the top cross braces into place on the side runners. The groove in the runners faces the inside. Turn the unit over and tap the bottom cross braces into place.

NOTE: *When stacking drawer systems, build one frame without the top cross braces, then tap the L connectors into the bottom of a second frame, and into the top of the first frame. Slide the stacked system into the closet. Do not install casters.*

Snap the floor protector caps onto the ends of the four Ts on the bottom. If you are going to use casters, tap leg extensions onto each of the four Ts. Use a hammer to tap a caster mounting bracket into the end of each leg extension. Use an open end wrench (or pair of pliers) to secure a caster into each caster mounting bracket. Turn the unit upright. Slide the drawers into the runners. Snap a drawer stop over each runner that contains the top of a drawer. The stop goes at the rear of the unit. You can purchase a top for the unit if desired. Simply snap the top onto the cross braces. Finally, roll the drawer system into place in the storage room or closet.

Install Hooks

There are many varieties of hooks on the market. What type you use depends on the types of items you plan to hang. A sweat suit or pair of jeans will require only a very simple, lightweight hook. Belts and ties may hang best from hooks specially designed for them. Determine which type of hook or hooks best suits your needs and then purchase them accordingly.

When installing, first determine the exact location the hooks will need to be hung, depending upon the item to be hung, and then install per the manufacturer's instruction.

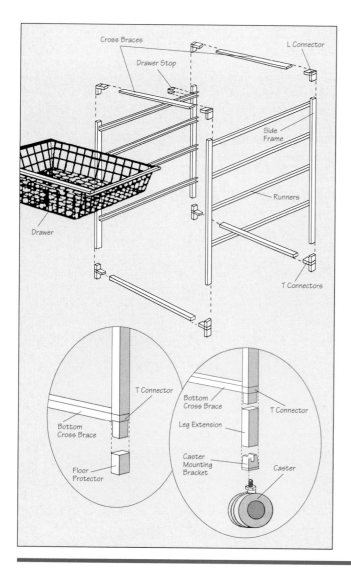

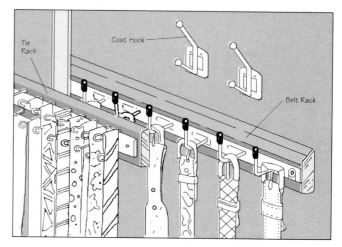

Building Techniques Guide

Although you do not have to be an expert to construct a closet from scratch, there are many construction techniques in which you will need to be familiar. You may already know how to accomplish many of the required tasks. If you are uncertain, use this chapter as an instructional guide to assist you in completing each step of the project successfully. As you proceed through a project certain steps will refer you to specific pages in this section of the book. Once again, you may discover that you are already familiar with the technique as many are common knowledge. If not, read the specific section referred to for more detailed instructions. Then, return to the original project.

Toenail Studs to Plates

"Toenailing" is the term used for joining two boards by nailing at an angle through the end or toe of one board into another. It is required for nailing studs to top or bottom plates that are already in place.

Hold the nail against the side of the stud, about 1½" away from the plate. Keep the nail at a 60- to 75-degree angle to the stud. Tap the nail until it is started, then pull it up so that it is at a 30- to 45-degree angle to the stud. Move your hand and drive the nail until it is flush with the stud.

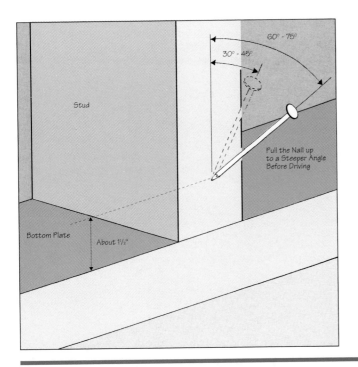

Install Top Plate

Before nailing the top plate into place, you must determine which way the ceiling joists run. A quick look in the attic should let you know. Otherwise, use an electric stud finder to determine their locations. If the joists are perpendicular to the new closet wall, proceed with nailing the top plate. If they are parallel to the new wall, and the new wall does not fall directly on a ceiling joist, blocking will have to be added in the attic. The blocking provides a nailing surface (refer to page 116). Nail the top plate into the ceiling joists (or blocking), two 12d nails into each joist. Then, toenail end studs from the Ts placed in the existing walls to the top plate. Use one toenail each side.

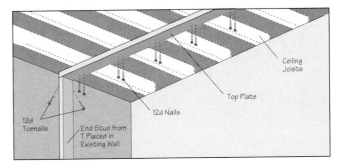

Install Bottom Plate

Set the bottom plate in place; carefully aligned between the chalk lines you have snapped on the floor. For wood floors, nail the bottom plate with 12d nails. Do not nail through the area of a rough opening for a door (if there is one) since this part of the bottom plate will be cut and removed. For concrete floors, use concrete nails. However, if the concrete is too hard, rent a power gun for shooting special hardened nails (pins) into concrete. Once the bottom plate is firmly nailed to the floor, toenail the end studs (on the Ts previously placed on existing walls) into the bottom plate. Use one toenail in each side.

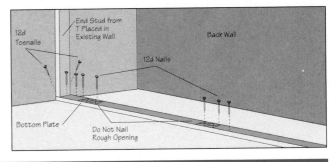

Build & Install a T

A T is an assembly of lumber designed to tie two frame walls together and provide nailing surfaces for the edges of finish material. When tying a new wall to an existing wall, you will need to construct the T differently than when both walls are new—to avoid damaging finish material on the existing wall.

If there is an existing stud within the cutaway area, add a second stud beside it and toenail top and bottom with 12d nails. Using 12d nails every 12", nail a third stud against the edges of the other two. The third stud should be within the chalk lines for the new wall, and will be the end stud of the wall.

Existing Wall: If there is no stud in the cutaway area, a different approach must be taken. Carefully measure the distance from the top surface of the bottom plate to the bottom surface of the top plate in the existing wall. Cut a 2x6 and a 2x4 to this length. Join the two pieces of lumber using 12d nails every 12". Use two nails at the top and bottom and stagger the nails from side to side in between. The 2x6 should extend 1" beyond the 2x4 on both sides.

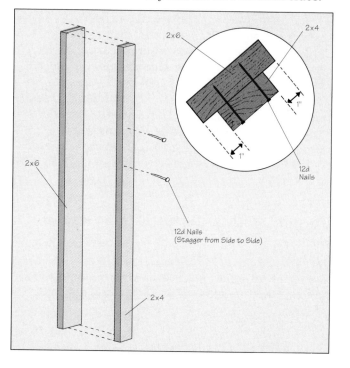

Measure 1½" from the front side of the existing bottom plate and draw a line parallel to the plate. Repeat at the top plate (installation is the same). Nail a 6" strip of 2x2 on the opposite side of the line with 12d nails at top and bottom. Slide the T into position. Toenail the T to the top and bottom plates with 12d nails.

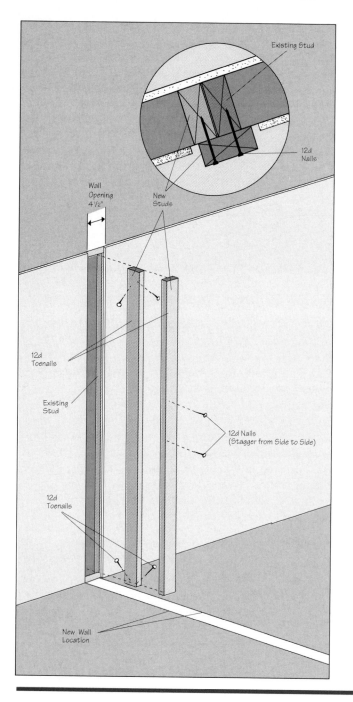

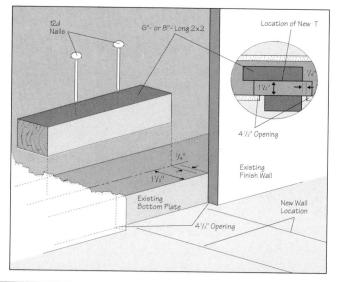

New Walls: If both walls are new, the T is built in the standard configuration, consisting of three studs and three pieces of blocking. If you are building walls that are standard height, build the T from precut studs. If not, cut the studs to the necessary length.

Cut three pieces of 2x4 blocking to a minimum of 12" long.

Lay a stud on top of the three pieces of blocking and nail together with 12d nails, three nails in each piece of blocking (see illustration). Turn the assembly on its side. Set a second stud on top of the edges of the three pieces of blocking. Temporarily use another piece of 2x4 beneath the stud to balance it. Nail the second stud to the blocking with 12d nails, three into each piece of blocking. Turn the assembly over and nail the third stud in the same manner as the second.

Build an L for a New Wall

An L is needed where two walls intersect and end at the intersection. The standard L is built using three studs and three pieces of blocking. If you are building standard height walls, make the L from precut studs. If not, cut the studs to the necessary length. Cut three pieces of 2x4 blocking to a minimum of 12" long. Lay a stud on top of the three pieces of blocking, all face down, and nail together with 12d nails, three nails each piece of blocking. Turn the assembly over and place a second stud on the opposite side of the blocking. Again, nail together using three 12d nails at each piece of blocking. Lay the assembly on its side. Place the third stud on the side of the assembly, aligned with one edge. This stud is the short leg of the L. Nail together with 12d nails every 12".

NOTE: *In some cases, the short leg of the L is not installed at this time. It is installed as part of an intersecting wall at a later point. Be sure you know the short leg is needed at this time before adding it.*

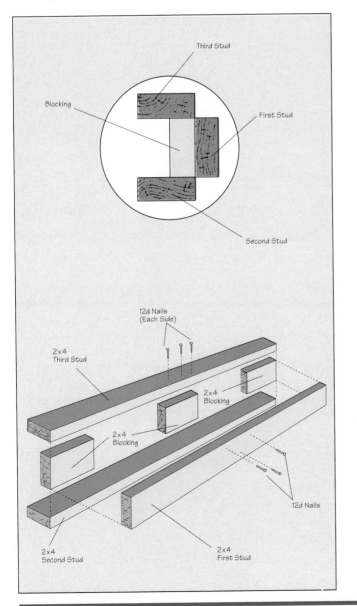

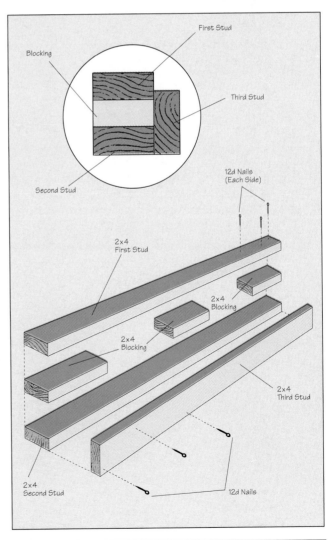

Add Blocking in the Attic

If the new wall will be parallel to the ceiling joists, but it will not fall directly beneath a joist, you will need to add blocking between the joists to provide a nailing surface for the top plate of the new wall. In one-story houses or the top story of multistory houses, the joists should be accessible from the attic.

At each end of the location for the new wall, hammer a nail up through the ceiling. The nails should be roughly in the center of the new wall location. Go into the attic and locate the nails.

CAUTION: If you have to remove insulation to find the nails, wear rubber gloves to protect your hands. Move the insulation out of the way carefully, so that you don't injure yourself on the exposed tips of the nails. Also, if there is no walking surface in the attic, nail sheets of 1/2" or thicker plywood or particleboard to the joists so that you can walk around without fear of falling through the ceiling. (Use 5/8" or 3/4" material if the ceiling joists are wider than 16" apart.) Lay the plywood perpendicular to the joists and use 8d nails every 16" on all sides. Make sure you do not cover joists where blocking will be installed.

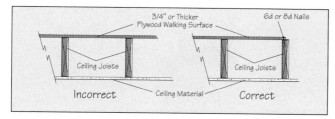

Starting at one of the nails, measure and mark every 24" on the ceiling joists on either side until you reach the second nail. Number each pair of marks directly on the top of the joists. Measure the distance between the ceiling joists at each of the marks and make a note of the number and the measurement. (If the measurements do not vary numbering is not necessary.) Cut pieces of 2x4 to the noted lengths. Write the number of each piece directly on the wood.

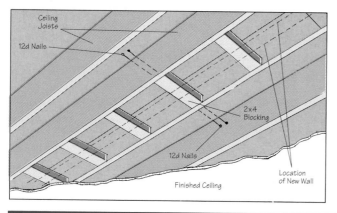

Set the blocks into place according to their numbers. Nail each piece with four 12d nails, two at each end. Nail through the opposite side of the joists and into the blocking. Avoid damaging the finish material on the ceiling below.

It may be a little easier to install the blocks if you first lay a 1x6 on top of the ceiling material directly above the location of the new wall. The 2x4 blocking goes on top of the 1x6. Carefully, nail the blocking to the 1x6 with a few 6d nails just to keep the 1x6 from moving. This method raises the blocking off the ceiling material, making it easier to nail the blocking to the joists. It also provides a continuous nailing surface for the top plate as well as an additional nailing surface on each side for the ceiling finish material if necessary.

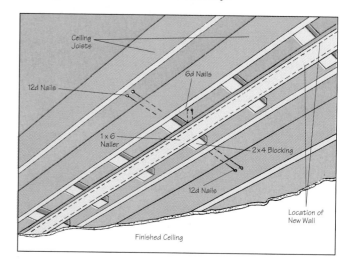

In places where the ceiling joists are not accessible and, in older homes that have lath-and-plaster ceilings, use toggle bolts and large washers to secure the top plate to the ceiling. Set the wall in place between the chalk lines. At 16" intervals, drill holes, large enough for a toggle bolt, all the way through the top plate, and finish material. Place the washer, then the toggle, onto the bolt and push it through the hole until the toggle opens above the ceiling material. Tighten the bolt to secure the toggle.

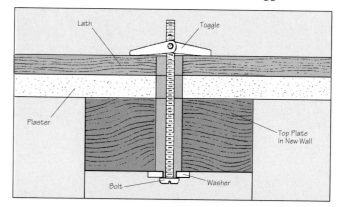

Identify Load-Bearing Walls

Before an existing wall can be removed, you must determine if the wall is a load-bearing wall. If so, the wall cannot be removed without installing another object to carry the load. A load-bearing wall carries the weight of a higher part of the structure and transfers it to a lower part of the structure. A nonbearing wall is a partition built solely for the purpose of dividing interior space.

All exterior walls are bearing walls. If your roof was built with prefabricated trusses, the interior walls are probably nonbearing walls. In most houses there is one interior bearing wall (though it may be in more than one section) that travels the length of the house. Since ceiling joists cannot usually span the full distance from the front to the back of the house, they rest on the interior bearing wall, thus diverting part of the ceiling load to the wall. To determine which wall carries the load, check either the attic or the basement or crawlspace or both. If you are not certain, consult an architect, reputable contractor or structural engineer. In some cases, your local building department will be able to make the determination for you.

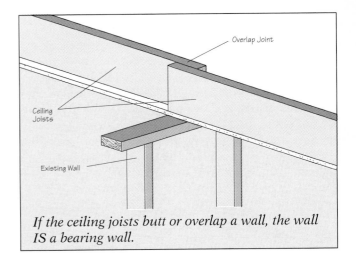

If the ceiling joists butt or overlap a wall, the wall IS a bearing wall.

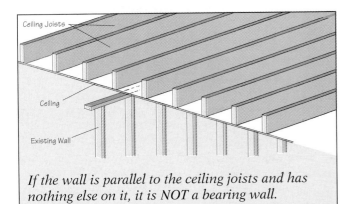

If the wall is parallel to the ceiling joists and has nothing else on it, it is NOT a bearing wall.

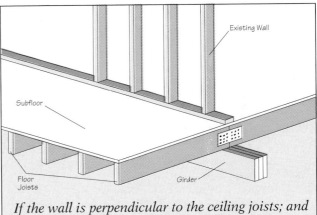

If the wall is perpendicular to the ceiling joists; and there is no back-beam above the wall; and the ceiling joists are continuous, chances are the wall is not a bearing wall. But this is not certain. If the wall is perpendicular to the floor joists and there is a girder beneath, the wall IS a bearing wall.

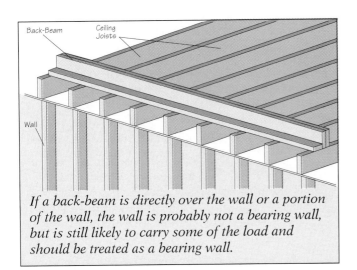

If a back-beam is directly over the wall or a portion of the wall, the wall is probably not a bearing wall, but is still likely to carry some of the load and should be treated as a bearing wall.

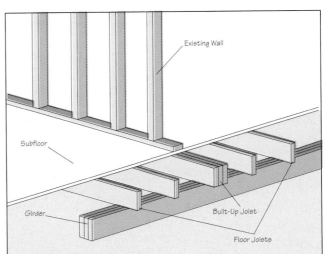

If the wall is parallel to the floor joists and there is a double or larger joist directly beneath the wall, the wall IS a bearing wall.

Install a Beam to Replace a Bearing Wall

Before a bearing wall can be removed, there must be an alternate means for carrying the load supported by the wall. This is done by installing a beam that diverts the load to its ends. The end must rest directly above a bearing wall. There are two ways to install a beam. One is an exposed beam and the other is a back-beam in the attic. If your project involves making alterations to a bearing wall, contact a structural engineer, architect or contractor for specific requirements.

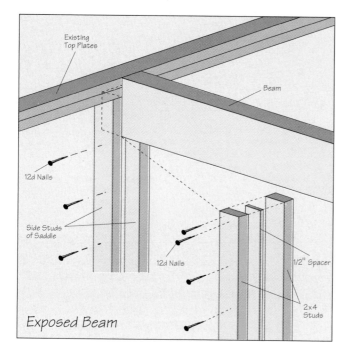

Exposed Beam

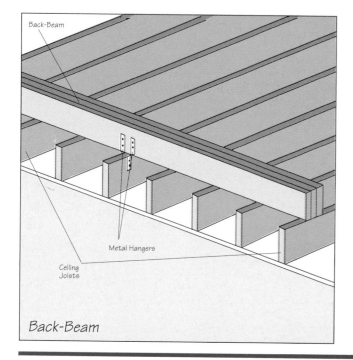

Back-Beam

Remove Wall Finish Material

Removing a wall is not as simple as taking a sledge hammer and knocking it down. Different materials require different methods of removal. Also, several different utility lines may be within a wall. Puncturing a gas line could be fatal!

First remove any trim. Outline the rough openings with masking tape to protect the surface material that is to remain.

For gypsum wallboard (drywall) cut along the edges (corners) of the wall to be removed with a utility knife. Make several cutting strokes until you go all the way through the board. Pull the drywall away from the studs with your hands. If you can't get a grip, use a hammer to make grip holes.

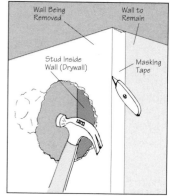

For plaster use a masonry chisel to cut as deep as possible, then crumble the plaster by hitting it with a hammer. When all the plaster is broken up, clean the room before starting on the lath. It will be easier to clean the two waste materials separately. Cut along the edges of the lath with a handsaw. (Be sure to check for utility lines first.) Pry the lath away from the studs with a crowbar.

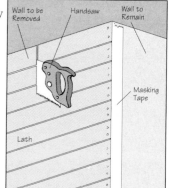

CAUTION: *Wear goggles and a mask when removing lath and plaster or drywall. A considerable amount of dust will be raised. Power tools are not recommended because they will only increase the dust and, in this case, are difficult to use without placing yourself in danger.*

For paneling, a handsaw or power saw can be used to cut along the rough opening. Set the depth of the saw blade to the thickness of the paneling so that you do not cut through any utility lines that may be in the wall. After cutting, pry the paneling off the studs with a crowbar.

CAUTION: *If the wall is a bearing wall, do NOT remove any studs until you install a beam. Without the beam, removing studs could cause a portion of the roof to collapse.*

Construct Door Header

Cut two pieces of 2x4 fit between the king studs. Then, cut a strip of 1/2"-thick material (plywood or particleboard) 1" shorter than the length of the 2x4s, and 3" wide. Nail the three pieces together with 12d nails. Place the header on top of the jack studs. Nail through the king studs and into the ends of the header with 12d nails. For bearing walls use 2x6s for doors under 3' wide and 2x8s for doors 3'-6' wide.

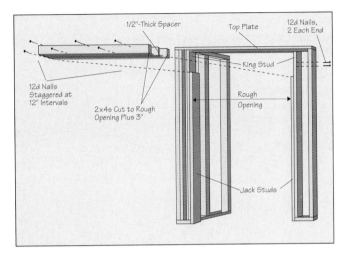

Install Cripple Studs Above Header

Cripple studs are added between the door header and top plate to provide a nailing surface for wall finish materials. Measure 16 3/4" from one of the side walls and place a mark on top of the header. From there, measure in 16" increments. Each time the 16" increment falls on top of the header, mark the location. Draw perpendicular lines through the marks and write an X on the side of each line closest to the side wall from which you started measuring. Repeat the process on the top plate, measuring from the same side wall. Measure between each set of marks and cut a cripple to fit. Toenail cripples with 8d nails.

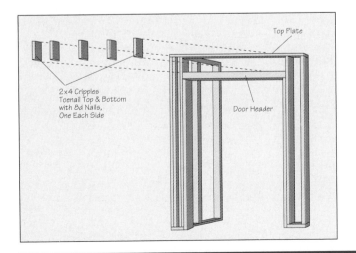

Select Closet Doors

Virtually any type of door can be used for a standard closet, although wider openings generally require some type of bi-fold or by-pass (sliding) door. Louvered and mirrored doors provide additional functions: Louvers allow the closet to "breathe" while mirrors provide full-length viewing for getting dressed.

Install Prehung Doors

Those of you who are not expert painters may wish to finish the door at this point and touch it up after installation.

For certain applications, such as kneewall closets in an attic, standard doors will be too tall. Flush doors can be shortened to fit. Louvered or paneled doors cannot be cut, but are available in shorter heights.

Remove the trim assembly from the prehung door. For bi-fold or by-pass doors, remove the doors from the frame (if they did not come separately). For a standard swinging door, leave the door in the frame but remove the temporary nails that hold the door in place.

Cut the two sides of the door frame to fit the height of the rough opening. Set the frame into the rough opening, centering the top in the opening. Carefully level the top of the frame. It is very important that the frame is level. It should be 1/2" above the subfloor for carpet and 1/8" above the subfloor for vinyl. For wood floors, adjust the frame to the thickness of the flooring. Add shims between the header and door frame on each side and tack the top into place with 10d finishing nails, one each side. For swinging doors, the nails should go

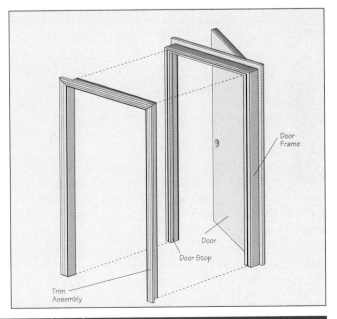

through the door stop and should NOT be driven all the way in at this time. For bi-fold or by-pass doors the nails should go generally in the center of the frame and can be driven flush when you are completely satisfied that the door frame is level.

Vertically level the hinge side of the door frame first (either side for bi-fold or by-pass) and secure with three nails, one at the top, one at the bottom, and one generally in the center. Use shims between the jack stud and door frame. Check for level at several points along the sides of the frame to make sure it is not bowed. Again, for standard swinging doors the nails should go through the door stop and should not be driven in all the way. Repeat on the other side of the frame.

If installing a standard swinging door, close the door and test for fit. If the door does not close easily and has an even seam all the way around, the frame is out of level. Adjust as necessary until the door closes properly. This can be done by making the shims thicker or thinner, or adding shims in additional

places for frames that bow or curve.

Once the frame is level and secure, add shims and 10d finishing nails every 12" all the way around. Begin with the hinge side. Nail close, but do not strike the wood. Slide the trim that had been removed back into place in the door frame. (For some bi-fold and by-pass doors, the precut trim is installed one piece at a time. Start with the top, then nail the sides into place.) Nail the trim every 12" with 4d finishing nails. Again, do not strike the wood. Use two nail punches,

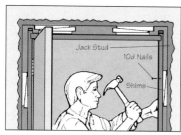

one for 10d nails, another for 4d nails, to set all the nails slightly below the surface of the wood. If the door is to be painted, fill the nail holes with wood putty first, then paint (or touch up if the door was already painted). If the door is to be stained, the stain should be applied first, then fill the holes using a matching color putty stick.

Install Bi-Fold Doors

Once the frame is in place and level, install the door track at the top of the frame per the manufacturer's directions. The mounting hardware is usually included. Following instructions, install the bottom door brackets at the bottom of each side; then install the alignment stops on the doors. Set the doors into the track at the top and brackets at the bottom. (The actual hardware and the amount of installation required will vary from manufacturer to manufacturer.)

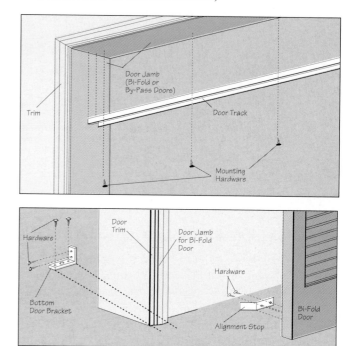

Install By-Pass Doors

Once the frame is in place and level, install the door track at the top of the frame per the manufacturer's directions. The mounting hardware is usually included. Following directions, install the door guide at floor level, centered between the sides. Set the doors into the track at the top and guide at the bottom. (The actual hardware and the amount of installation required will vary from manufacturer to manufacturer.)

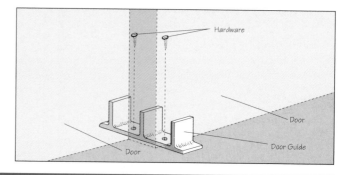

Install Drywall

To minimize the joints that must be taped, use the following chart to determine the drywall nailing pattern (based on a standard 8' ceiling):

Wall Width	Drywall Size	Sheet Placement
4' and under	4x8	Vertical
4'+ to 8'	4x8	Horizontal
8'+ and over	4x12	Horizontal

Measure the walls and draw the pattern on paper before nailing drywall. Remember, the goals are to minimize the joints that will require finishing and to keep the majority of the joints at a comfortable working height. For a wall that is mostly made up of the door opening, you may wish to cut the strips of drywall first, then nail into place. This will reduce the amount of drywall needed and could reduce the length of joints to be finished.

Rerouting Electric or Water Lines

CAUTION: *Do NOT try to reroute gas lines. Accidents could be fatal. Gas lines should be handled only by a professional.*

With the wall material removed, reroute any utility lines present inside the wall. Electrical lines can be changed so that they are routed over new doors instead of through them. Turn off the power at the circuit box and check lines with a voltage tester to be positive that there is no power before removing them. Remove the cable from the outlet box at one end. Pull the cable through the holes in the studs. Drill a hole, just large enough for the cable, through the bottom of each rafter directly above a kneewall or through cripple studs above a door. Route the wire through the new holes and reconnect. If the cable is not long enough, disconnect at both ends, discard and install a new length of the same type cable.

Water lines are not as simple. If you are going to do this type of work yourself, refer to Creative Homeowner Press® *Modern Home Plumbing* by Mort Schultz. When relocating water lines, turn off the water at the meter before starting.

CAUTION: *Do not try to reroute drain pipes. A mistake could cause the line to cease flowing properly. Enlist the services of a professional if you have a gravity flow line to be moved.*

For Higher Ceilings: If the wall is 4' wide or less, cut 4x12 sheets to the ceiling height and install vertically. For walls taller than 8', place the sheets horizontally with one full sheet at the ceiling and another at the floor. Piece the drywall in the middle to put the extra joint at an easy working height for finishing.

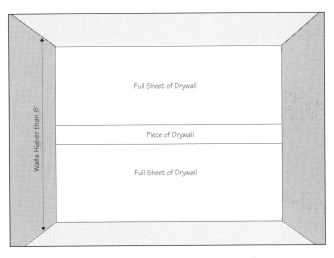

Cut & Nail Drywall

When cutting drywall, lay it on a raised flat surface with the face up. (Saw horses will work if you lay a sheet of plywood on top of them first.) Measure and mark the cut line on the drywall. Place a drywall T-square or a similar metal straightedge along the line to be cut. Score with a utility knife. Slide the drywall over so that the scored line is on the edge of the support, then snap the drywall back at the line. Finally, cut along the back paper with a utility knife.

For door cutouts, nail the full sheet of drywall into place first. Cut along the two sides. It will take several passes with a utility knife to cut all the way through. Using the utility knife, score the other line

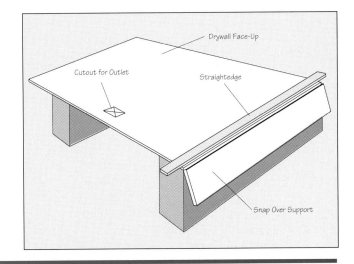

on the face of the drywall. Snap the drywall at the score, then cut the paper backing to remove the excess piece.

For electrical outlets and switches, measure and mark the location of the box on the front of the drywall. Using a utility knife, score the marked outline of the box, then cut an X within the box, connecting the corners. Tap the middle with a hammer until the drywall breaks away. Cut the backing paper to remove the pieces. You also can use a keyhole saw for cutting out electrical boxes, though it will take a little longer.

Once you have determined the drywall nailing pattern for your project, raise the sheets in place and nail with drywall (ring shank) nails. Place the nails approximately 12" apart around the edges of the board and 16" apart on interior studs. Nail just far enough so that the surface of the drywall is dimpled, but the paper is not broken. For horizontal sheets, nail the top sheet first. This will help to avoid gaps at the top. The bottom sheet can be levered up snug against the top sheet. Any gap at the bottom will be hidden by baseboard.

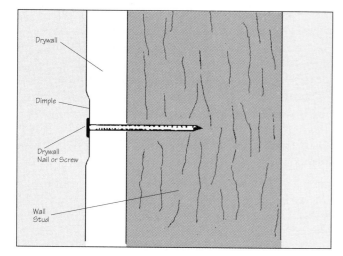

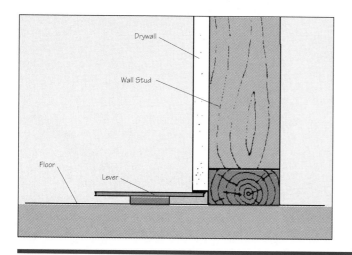

Finish Drywall

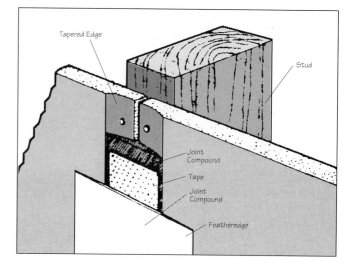

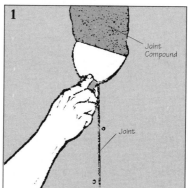

1. If using paper tape for the joints, apply a 4"- to 5"-wide filler coat of joint compound directly over the joint. Use a 6" taping knife. Fill the entire length of a single joint, one at a time.

2. Place paper tape on the filler coat and secure the top of the tape with a small portion of joint compound.

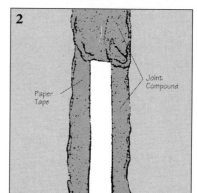

3. Embed the paper tape into the filler coat with a 6" taping knife. Start at the top of the joint and drag downward.

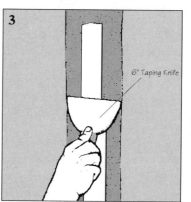

You can eliminate the filler coat by using a self-adhering mesh joint tape. The mesh in the tape allows the joint compound from the first coat to flow through. This is a relatively new item that makes finishing drywall a bit easier.

4. For inside corners, apply a 4" to 5"-wide filler coat of joint compound to both sides of the joint.

5. Fold the tape before placing it on the filler.

6. Place paper tape on the filler coat and secure at the top with joint compound. Embed the paper tape into the filler coat with a 6" taping knife.

7. On outside corners, install a metal corner bead using drywall nails or screws. The bead is needed to support and protect the corner joint. Holes in the bead allow joint compound to flow behind for added strength.

8. With all joints taped, apply the first coat of joint compound. On inside corners apply a 5"- to 6"-wide coat of compound on one side only. For outside corners, apply a 5"- to 6"-wide coat to both sides. For flat joints apply a 6" to 8" coat of compound.

9. Apply joint compound to all nail locations. This is difficult work for a novice, so don't get discouraged if it does not apply as evenly as you would like.

10. After applying joint compound to the wall, use the knife to remove the excess, smoothing the joint flush with the wall.

It will take from one to three days for joint compound to dry.

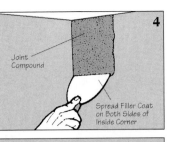

Joint Compound / Spread Filler Coat on Both Sides of Inside Corner

Fold Paper Tape

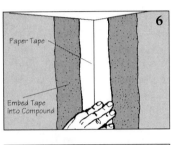

Paper Tape / Embed Tape into Compound

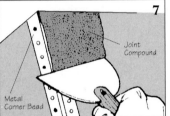

Metal Corner Bead / Joint Compound

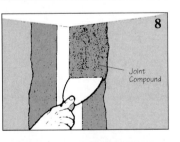

Joint Compound

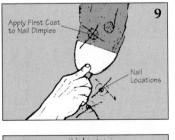

Apply First Coat to Nail Dimples / Nail Locations

Smooth Compound Flush with Joint

11. When thoroughly dry, sand very lightly with 80-grit sandpaper. Do NOT sand through to the tape or through the paper surface of the drywall.

12. After sanding apply a 5"- to 6"-wide coat of joint compound to the other side of all inside corners. Apply a 6" to 8" second coat to outside corners and a 12" to 14" coat to flat joints. Also apply a second coat to the nail locations. Apply the second coat as smoothly as possible.

13. When dry, wipe with a damp sponge. Sand lightly only if essential. Unless you are experienced with this type of work, a very light third coat may be required to achieve the greatest smoothness.

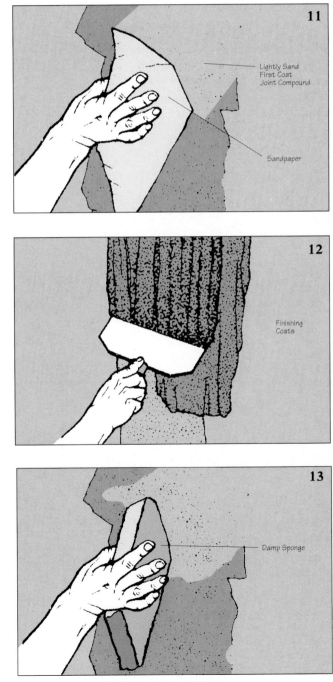

Lightly Sand First Coat Joint Compound / Sandpaper

Finishing Coats

Damp Sponge

Install 4x8 Paneling

To install paneling, start from the end of the wall where you began measuring for studs. Unless the walls are terribly out of plumb, the first sheet will not have to be cut. Set the sheet into place, level one side, and test for fit. A small gap in the corner where the paneling starts is alright since it will be covered with corner trim. The other edge should fall along the center of a stud. If the panel edge does not fall on a stud, try starting from the other end of the wall. If it fails both ways, the first sheet will have to be trimmed. If the wall is badly out of plumb, the top or bottom of each panel may need to be trimmed before installing. Otherwise, gaps at the top and bottom will be covered with crown molding and baseboard, respectively.

Mark for doors on the back of the paneling and snap chalk lines. Set on top of the sawhorses and cut with a circular saw. Be sure to keep the face down to avoid splintering on the finished side of the paneling. Keep the face up if using a handsaw.

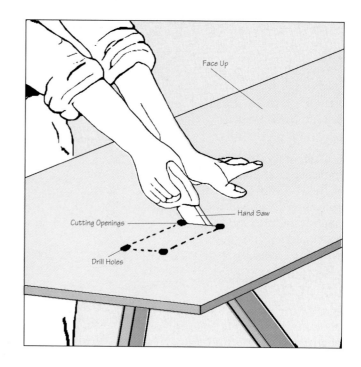

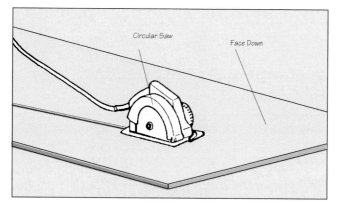

Nail each sheet of paneling into place with matching paneling nails that are the same color. If using particleboard, pegboard, plywood, or a similar sheet material you can nail with 4d finishing nails. If you prefer, panel adhesive can be used to glue the panels in place. Some nailing will be required to hold the panels while the glue cures. For the last sheet along the wall, measure from the end of the previous sheet to the wall at both top and bottom. There probably will be some variance. Mark the paneling, then saw and nail it into place to complete the wall.

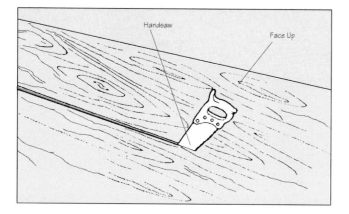

For electrical outlets and switches, place chalk line powder on the edges of the electrical box. Set the paneling in place and slap against the face of the drywall in the area of the electrical box. Lay the paneling on a pair of sawhorses with the face down. Drill a 3/4" hole in each corner of the box. Finish cutting the box with a keyhole or similar saw.

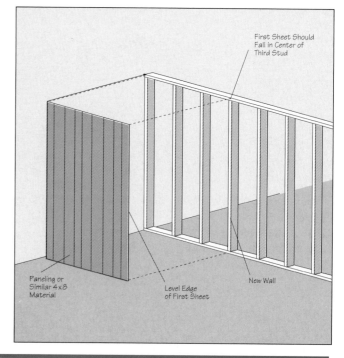

Install Baseboard Molding

Use baseboard that matches the style that already exists in the room. You will need to cut the baseboard to fit when joining two lengths together, and where it meets at inside corners, outside corners and door trim. Each situation requires a different cut.

When lengths of baseboard must be joined together cut the ends at 45-degree angles (never butt-flush cut ends together). Where baseboards meet at an outside corner cut each end at a 45-degree angle. Baseboard should be cut flush where it will butt against the door trim or an inside corner. When the baseboard meets the side wall baseboard, first make a flush cut and then cut at a 45-degree angle (with a miter saw) where the baseboard meets the side wall baseboard. Using a coping saw, trim along the edge of the 45-degree cut (see right).

Nail baseboard into place, using 6d finishing nails at each end and approximately every 16" between. (For very short pieces, set nails closer than 16". Drill nail holes through the baseboard before nailing into the wall). Keep the nails approximately 1" above the floor so that they will go into the bottom plate behind the wall finish material.

NOTE: *For carpeted floors, the baseboard should be raised 1/2" above the subfloor. Set the baseboard on pieces of 1/2" material before nailing.*

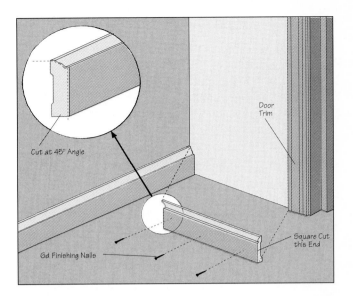

Install Crown Molding

Crown molding is installed where the wall meets the ceiling in the same manner as baseboard. The only difference is that there are no cuts for doors. Crown molding is usually needed when installing paneled walls.

Install Corner Molding

You will need inside corner trim at the corners. Select any inside corner and measure the distance from the top of the baseboard to the bottom of the crown molding (or the ceiling if not installing crown molding). Cut a piece of inside corner trim to the measured distance. Set in place and nail with 4d finishing nails approximately every 16". Repeat for the other inside corners. Outside corner trim is installed in the same manner.

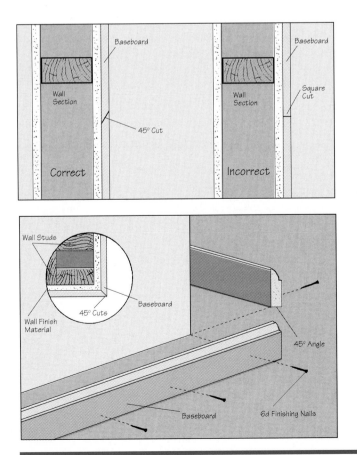

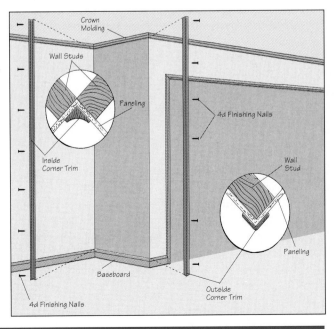

Install Cedar Boards in a Closet

For those who prefer cedar-lined closets, tongue-and-groove cedar closet lining can be purchased at most lumberyards. It usually is available by the lineal foot or prepackaged in bundles that cover a specified number of square feet. Usually, the cedar is nailed or glued over a finish material such as drywall. Cedar boards 1/4" thick or thicker can be nailed directly over studs.

Horizontal application is recommended, but you can install the boards vertically if you prefer. Vertical application will require blocking between the studs unless you are installing the boards over a wood finish material. Angled applications are less common because they result in greater waste.

If applying over a finished wall, locate the studs with a stud finder and snap chalk lines down the center of each stud. Start installing the cedar in the lower left corner of a wall. For a horizontal application, place the groove against the floor. If the ends of the board are tongue and grooved, the tongue should be on the right. For vertical applications, place the groove side against the adjacent wall with the grooved end to the floor. Nail the cedar in place with 4d finishing nails. The nails should go into the studs.

When the other side of the wall is reached, cut the tongue end of the board off. It can be used to start the next row. (Because the boards are tongue and grooved, the point where two pieces butt together does not have to be at a stud.) The best way to cut the boards is with a miter saw so that all cuts are perfectly straight. However, you can use a circular saw or crosscut saw. Continue adding rows until you reach the ceiling. The last row will probably require ripping the boards to fit. Once the first wall is finished, begin the adjacent wall on the right. Work clockwise until you return to the original wall. This will help make a better fit in the corners. You may elect to install four pieces of corner trim, if needed to cover gaps.

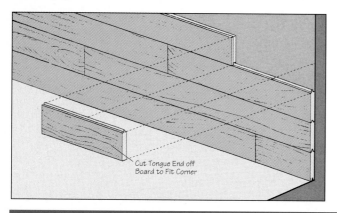

Cut Tongue End off Board to Fit Corner

Install Carpet

CAUTION: *If you are unsure about whether you can install or reinstall carpet without damaging it, hire a professional to do the job for you.*

If adding carpet in a new closet, nail a strip of tack board along the new wall. The tacks slope toward one side of the strip. This side should face the wall. Note that the strip is not installed against the wall, but about 1/2" away from it. Unroll and lay the carpet pad into place, cutting as necessary to cover the closet floor. The pad should lay inside the tack board and not on top of it.

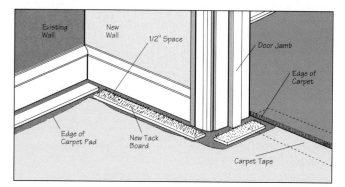

Cut the carpet slightly larger than the closet floor and lay it in place. Use a knee kicker to stretch the carpet over the tack strip on one side wall. At the opposite side wall, use a carpet knife to *carefully* cut the carpet where the floor meets the new wall. As you cut, lay the carpet down every few inches and check the cut. One mistake can ruin the carpet. Tighten the carpet with the knee kicker as you go. Use the carpet knife to press the carpet over the tack strip and down between the bottom of the baseboard and the subfloor.

If the closet is in a room that is already carpeted, trim the new carpet even with the existing carpet along the door opening. Slide a piece of seam tape under the two pieces of carpet and heat with a seaming iron. Carefully lay the carpet onto the tape, aligning the seam so the two pieces fit smoothly. Allow a few minutes for the melted plastic on the seam tape to cool and harden. Then use the knee kicker and carpet knife to install the carpet at the back closet wall.

Glossary

Back clip A plastic-coated metal hook attached to the wall, used for hanging plastic-coated wire organizer systems (baskets, shelves, etc.)

Baseboard A molding placed along the bottom of a wall to cover the gap between the wall and floor.

Beam Horizontal structural member that sits on posts or walls and supports the structure above it. When bearing walls are removed, they must be replaced by a beam.

Bearing wall (load-bearing wall) A wall designed to support rafters, ceiling joists or walls directly above it. All outside walls of a house are bearing walls.

Blocking Short pieces of lumber installed between joists or studs to provide a nailing surface for framing members; for example, when attaching the top plate of a new wall parallel to existing ceiling joists.

Coated-wire system A prefabricated closet organizer system whose components (shelves, baskets, shoe shelves, etc.) consist of plastic-coated wire. These systems require special hardware for installation.

Cripples In wall construction, short 2x4 blocks fitted between the header of an opening and the wall top plate to maintain the structural integrity of the wall and to provide nailing for wall covering materials.

Crown molding A decorative molding attached to a wall at ceiling height, usually used in conjunction with paneled walls.

Dado A slot cut in side wall of a shelving system into which the end of the shelf is inserted. Dados are usually cut with a router, mounted on a router table, or on a tablesaw equipped with a dado blade.

Drywall Also known as wallboard or gypsum board, a paper covered panel of compressed gypsum used as the primary wall covering in almost all homes. It can be finished to look like a plaster wall or used to support other wallcoverings.

Furring strips Narrow wood strips or cleats attached to the side wall of a shelving system to support shelves; also a narrow wood strip attached horizontally to a finished wall to

provide a nailing surface for fixtures, shelves or cabinets.

Header In wall framing, a horizontal structural member placed above a door or window opening to support the framing above it.

Heel stop A strip of wood (1x1 or smaller) attached to an angled shoe shelf; the shoe heels are hooked over the heel stop to keep the shoes from sliding off.

Integral rod and shelf Typically a prefabricated wire closet shelf with a rod built into the front edge for hanging clothes.

Jack studs In wall framing, partial studs fitted between the bottom plate and a door or window header; full-length studs adjacent to the jack studs are called king studs.

Joiner plate In coated-wire organizer systems, a piece of hardware used to attach support braces to coated-wire shelves.

Joint compound A thick, spreadable substance that dries hard and can be finished like plaster. It is used to fill the seams between sheets of drywall and for small repairs to damaged plaster or wallboard walls.

Joists Horizontal framing members in a floor or ceiling to which you attach the finish floor or ceiling materials. Joists are typically placed on 16" or 24" centers to provide nailing for 4'x8' panels of plywood or drywall.

King Studs In wall framing, a full-length stud fitted between the bottom plate of a door or window header.

Knee kicker A tool used for stretching carpet; the front end of the tool grips the carpet; the back end is shaped so the user can apply forward pressure with the knee.

L (for wall construction) A framing assembly that ties two walls together to form an outside corner.

Laminated system A prefabricated closet organizer system that is made up of components that consist of plastic laminated particleboard. Installation is usually manufacturer-specific.

Organizer system Any system of shelves, drawers, closet rods, baskets, etc. fitted into a closet to maximize

usable space. Such systems may be hand built or prefabricated.

Rabbet A square cutout in the end or edge of a board into which another board fits; commonly used in drawer construction.

Runners Horizontal members of a metal frame used to support coated-wire baskets or drawers. Prefabricated wire-basket drawer systems usually come in 4-, 7-, and 10-runner systems, depending on the size or number of baskets desired.

Screen molding Also known as cap molding, this molding consists of flat, narrow strips of fir or pine, with the top edges rounded over slightly. Traditionally used for attaching screening to wooden screen doors, screen molding can also be used to cover the exposed edges of plywood to provide a finished appearance for shelving systems.

Shelf tower A tall set of shelves with two vertical dividers, that fits into a closet; usually secured to the back wall with furring strips.

Studs In wall construction, vertical 2x4 framing members that fit between the top and bottom plates. Studs are usually placed at each end of the wall and on 16" or 24" centers to provide a nailing surface for standard 4x8 drywall sheets or paneling.

T (for wall construction) A framing assembly that ties two walls together at right angles—usually a new closet wall into an existing wall—so that finish materials may be applied to both sides of the wall. A variation of T framing is used to tie walls together at 45-degree angles.

Tackless strip A thin strip of wood or metal in which many small, sharp teeth are imbedded to grip the edges of a wall-to-wall carpet when they are hooked over the teeth. The strip is nailed down with the angled teeth pointing toward the wall; it inherits its name from the amount of tacking it eliminates from carpet installation.

Toenailing A nailing method used for joining the end of one board to the face of another by driving the nail through both pieces at an angle.

Conversion Charts

Dimensional Lumber

Nominal Size (You order) Inches	Actual Size (You get) Inches	Nominal Size (You order) Inches	Actual Size (You get) Inches
1 x 1	3/4 x 3/4	2 x 2	1¾ x 1¾
1 x 2	3/4 x 1½	2 x 3	1½ x 2½
1 x 3	3/4 x 2½	2 x 4	1½ x 3½
1 x 4	3/4 x 3½	2 x 6	1½ x 5½
1 x 6	3/4 x 5½	2 x 8	1½ x 7¼
1 x 8	3/4 x 7¼	2 x 10	1½ x 9¼
1 x 10	3/4 x 9¼	2 x 12	1½ x 11¼
1 x 12	3/4 x 11¼		

Metric Length

Lengths in Meters	Equivalent Feet and Inches	Lengths in Meters	Equivalent Feet and Inches
1.8m	5' 10⅞"	5.1m	16' 8¾"
2.1m	6' 10⅝"	5.4m	17' 8⅝"
2.4m	7' 10½"	5.7m	18' 8⅜"
2.7m	8' 10¼"	5.7m	18' 8⅜"
3.0m	9' 10⅛"	5.7m	18' 8⅜"
3.3m	10' 9⅞"	6.0m	19' 8¼"
3.6m	11' 9¾"	6.3m	20' 8"
3.9m	12' 9½"	6.6m	21' 7⅞"
4.2m	13' 9⅜"	6.9m	22' 7⅝"
4.5m	14' 9⅓"	7.2m	23' 7½"
4.8m	15' 9"	7.5m	24' 7¼"
		7.8m	25' 7⅛"

All the dimensions are based on 1 inch = 25 mm

Lumber

Sizes: Metric cross-sections are so close to their nearest Imperial sizes, as noted below, that for most purposes they may be considered equivalents.

Lengths: Metric lengths are based on a 300mm module, which is slightly shorter in length than an Imperial foot. It will, therefore, be important to check your requirements accurately to the nearest inch and consult the table below to find the metric length required.

Areas: The metric area is a square meter. Use the following conversion factors when converting from Imperial data: 100 sq. feet=9,290 sq. meters.

Metric Sizes Shown Before Nearest Imperial Equivalent

millimeters	inches	millimeters	inches	millimeters	inches
16 x 75	5/8 x 3	32 x 225	1¼ x 9	63 x 100	2½ x 4
16 x 100	5/8 x 4	32 x 250	1¼ x 10	63 x 125	2½ x 5
16 x 125	5/8 x 5	32 x 300	1¼ x 12	63 x 150	2½ x 6
16 x 150	5/8 x 6			63 x 175	2½ x 7
		38 x 75	1½ x 3	63 x 200	2½ x 8
19 x 75	3/4 x 3	38 x 100	1½ x 4	63 x 225	2½ x 9
19 x 100	3/4 x 4	38 x 125	1½ x 5		
19 x 125	3/4 x 5	38 x 150	1½ x 6	75 x 100	3 x 4
19 x 150	3/4 x 6	38 x 175	1½ x 7	75 x 125	3 x 5
		38 x 200	1½ x 8	75 x 150	3 x 6
22 x 75	7/8 x 3	38 x 225	1½ x 9	75 x 175	3 x 7
22 x 100	7/8 x 4			75 x 200	3 x 8
22 x 125	7/8 x 5	44 x 75	1¾ x 3	75 x 225	3 x 9
22 x 150	7/8 x 6	44 x 100	1¾ x 4	75 x 250	3 x 10
		44 x 125	1¾ x 5	75 x 300	3 x 12
25 x 75	1 x 3	44 x 150	1¾ x 6		
25 x 100	1 x 4	44 x 175	1¾ x 7	100 x 100	4 x 4
25 x 125	1 x 5	44 x 200	1¾ x 8	100 x 150	4 x 6
25 x 150	1 x 6	44 x 225	1¾ x 9	100 x 200	4 x 8
25 x 175	1 x 7	44 x 250	1¾ x 10	100 x 250	4 x 10
25 x 200	1 x 8	44 x 300	1¾ x 12	100 x 300	4 x 12
25 x 225	1 x 9				
25 x 250	1 x 10	50 x 75	2 x 3	150 x 150	6 x 6
25 x 300	1 x 12	50 x 100	2 x 4	150 x 200	6 x 8
		50 x 125	2 x 5	150 x 300	6 x 12
		50 x 150	2 x 6		
32 x 75	1¼ x 3	50 x 175	2 x 7		
32 x 100	1¼ x 4	50 x 200	2 x 8	200 x 200	8 x 8
32 x 125	1¼ x 5	50 x 225	2 x 9	250 x 250	10 x 10
32 x 150	1¼ x 6	50 x 250	2 x 10	300 x 300	12 x 12
32 x 175	1¼ x 7	50 x 300	2 x 12		
32 x 200	1¼ x 8				

Index